SUBJECT RELATIONS

SUBJECT RELATIONS

UNCONSCIOUS EXPERIENCE AND RELATIONAL PSYCHOANALYSIS

Naomi G. Rucker, Ph.D.
Karen L. Lombardi, Ph.D.

ROUTLEDGE
New York and London

Published in 1998

Routledge
29 West 35th Street
New York, NY 10001

Published in Great Britain by

Routledge
11 New Fetter Lane
London EC4P 4EE

Library of Congress Cataloging-in-Publication Data

Rucker, Naomi, 1954–
    Subject relations : Unconscious experience and relational
psychoanalysis / Naomi Rucker, Karen Lombardi.
        p.   cm.
    Includes bibliographical references and index.
    ISBN 0–415–91422–1.   —   ISBN 0–415–91423–X (pbk.)
    1. Psychoanalysis.   I. Lombardi, Karen, 1945–   .   II. Title.
BF173.R79   1997
150.19′5—dc21   97–16984
                                                         CIP

CONTENTS

ACKNOWLEDGMENTS

We would like jointly to acknowledge a number of people whose contributions have enriched this work. Our special appreciation is extended to Maureen MacGrogan, who first recognized the promise of this book and gave us the courage to continue with it. We only regret that she was unable to see this project through to its end. Also deserving thanks are Heidi Freund, our current editor, and the editorial and production assistants who helped bring this book to completion. They have been most encouraging and facilitative. We also thank Estelle Shane, Ph.D., whose intelligent discussion of our ideas pushed us to develop them further, and Carol Bivens-Levin, whose thoughtful and professional editorial comments improved the clarity and precision of our presentation. Warren Wilner, Ph.D., has been, for both of us, a source of unique perspectives that have captivated our attention and enlivened our ideas. Over the years, Dr. Wilner has touched us with his imagination, intellect, perspicacious humor, and many flashes of brilliance.

To each other, we express gratitude and appreciation for the many years of friendship and professional collaboration that have brought us to this mutual endeavor. We have richly enhanced one another's thinking and development. Our intuitive sense of liking and being like the other have cultivated a closeness in feeling and in intellect that have allowed this project to flourish. We have done well with each other's quirks and we enjoy and, hopefully, complement each other's talents. Neither of us could have written this book without the other.

The following chapters originally found a forum at the Annual Meetings of Division 39 (Psychoanalysis) of the American Psychological Association, being presented there in earlier forms: Chapter 1—Resurrecting the Unconscious in Contemporary Psychoanalysis; Chapter 3—Sounds of Silence: Parallel Dreaming and the Mutual Dream; Chapter 5—The Mutual Creation of Temporal Experience; Chapter 6—The Prenatal Anlage of Psychic Life; Chapter 7—Subject Relations as Seen through Prenatal Observation; Chapter 8—Mother as Object, Mother as Subject.

In addition to our joint acknowledgements, each of us would like to recognize particular persons individually.

N.R.: The single most personal influence on the scholarly dimension of my professional life has been Karen Lombardi. She has been a kindred intellectual spirit who, perhaps without knowing it, has given me much of the confidence in my ideas that I now enjoy. From another domain, I am particularly indebted to the writings of Harold Searles and Ignacio Matte-Blanco, who greatly influenced and helped crystallize my thinking. I also am grateful to my patients, who have given me the opportunity to experience so many dimensions of relatedness.

The following individuals have been distinctive in my life, and their meaning[fulness] to me is threaded through the pages of this book. Two of these people are no longer alive, but their spirits have guided my hand. I would like to honor the following people: my parents, James ("Bunny") and Helen, whose uncommon lives and ideas continually inspire me to explore outside the lines; my children, Philip and Clara, whose extraordinary and ordinary presence balances me there; and Rosemary Creed Lukton, who, in her gentle specialness, first brought unconscious experience to life for me.

K.L.: My ways of thinking have been most profoundly influenced by:

My analyst and the process of analysis.

My students and the ways in which they have taught me and affected my teaching.

My patients and the deepening experiences of both intimacy and alienation that are at the heart of this book.

A separate thanks is deserved by those who have influenced this work both directly and indirectly, including Lawrence Balter, Joseph Newirth, Michael Civin, Linda Jacobs, Eva Lapidos, Drucilla Cornell, and to those more distant, but no less significant, intellectual foreparents Harold Searles, Heinrich Racker, Melanie Klein, Sandor Ferenczi, D. W. Winnicott, and Ignacio Matte-Blanco. I also extend my gratitude to those of my students who have contributed directly to this book: Lisa Jepsen, Rachel Karliner, Frances Roper, and Dalia Gold. Thanks to my father-in-law Paul Civin, a theoretical mathematician who understands many languages, and my mother-in-law Harriet Civin for their unflagging interest in this project, and to my Sarah Lawrence compatriots past and present, Claudia Hartley and Mary Crocker Fassett, for their confidence in my ways of thinking. I wish to express my loving appreciation to my mother, Theresa, and remembrance of my father, Louis, for their contributions to my development.

Naomi Rucker has been my psychic and intellectual comrade since we first met during our analytic training. My husband, Michael Civin, and my daughter, Chloë, have lived this book with me in a continuous interplay of symmetrical and asymmetrical experiences. It is through them that I know.

Preface

The problem of the One and the Many, of multiplicity and unity, has been present in every period of Western thought. Ancient philosophers and metaphysicists such as Spinoza, Plato, and Aristotle addressed questions of Oneness and Being with particular vigor, but related controversies over the unity and divisibility of space, time, or matter occupy the attention of modern as well as ancient thinkers. Almost every fundamental conception of humankind is influenced by one's position on this singular philosophical problem. Issues of unity and multiplicity pervade human experience and mentation and seem integral to our very presence on this earth.

As individual beings, we all come into existence through the uniting of sperm and egg, the bringing together of two entities, whole within themselves, to create, synergistically, a third entity that is simultaneously neither and both of its components. Each human being is a whole made up of parts, each part being both whole within itself and composed of other parts. All of these whole/part elements create a structure, a function, an experience that is both unified and discrete. Thus, our essential wholeness and our essential multiplicity are embedded within the nature of being alive, coexisting in dialectical tension with each other, such that they can be seen as simultaneously separable and inseparable. Joined like points on a Mobius strip, rather than opposed like ends of a continuum, expressions of Oneness and Many develop in convoluted and infinitely fluctuating relationship to one another while maintaining their essential form.

To see the universe as both unified and divided, existing in dialectical tension, requires an outlook that cannot be articulated readily. The meanings and implications of such a perspective are larger, more encompassing than the language that we have available, and perhaps larger than our mental capacity to grasp them. These ideas are of us, but perhaps we are also of them. In this book, we have attempted to elucidate the meaningfulness of a synergistic and dialectical conception of psychic life. We have not answered the questions posed by the problem of the unity and multiplicity, but we have begun to articulate the nature of these questions as they apply to unconscious experience and psychic relatedness. The realm of unconscious relational experience in psychoanalysis holds infinite potential for exploration of the universal and omnipresent enigma of the One and the Many.

Subject Relations is, itself, both one and many. The organization of *Subject Relations* allows it to be read in totality or to be perused in more selective fashion. Once the initial two chapters are understood, each subsequent chapter can be read independently. The opening chapters address the position of the concept of the unconscious in contemporary psychoanalysis, describe Matte-Blanco's set theory of the unconscious, present a revised conception of identificatory processes in the context of unconscious relatedness, and introduce the constructs of subject relations and the related unconscious. The central ideas in these introductory chapters scaffold subject-relations theory and are critical to understanding the clinical and nonclinical expositions that follow, but each of Chapters 3–11 offers a topical exploration of relational subjectivity that otherwise can stand alone. Because an understanding of Matte-Blanco's ideas is critical to an appreciation of a subject-relational perspective, constructs of set theory relevant to subject relations are discussed at length in the text of this book and a summary of these constructs is available as an Appendix.

Subject Relations is our mutual endeavor. Yet, it is also the culmination of our individual journeys, and of the relatedness that has evolved between us. It represents our synergistic creative process. In this endeavor, we have been both together and apart, and have written jointly and separately. The task of synthesizing our togetherness and our apartness has resulted in the whole, made up of parts, that you, the reader, are about to read. The ideas in *Subject Relations* will press you to relinquish the linear logic that characterizes usual intellectual thought and to be absorbed in an intellectual experience in which ideas are both dense, and intangible and evanescent. It is hoped that you will not just understand our book, but have the experience of being of it.

—Naomi Rucker, Ph.D.
—Karen Lombardi, Ph.D.

1

RESURRECTING THE UNCONSCIOUS IN CONTEMPORARY PSYCHOANALYSIS

Karen Lombardi

Both modern Freudians and those groups loosely affiliated under the rubric of relational theory have a problematic relationship with the concept of the unconscious. The unconscious, once so central to psychoanalytic theory, now tends to be relegated to secondary or even tertiary importance by both relational and drive theorists. The unconscious is of interest to both groups insofar as it is seen as the location of distortion or dissociation of conscious experience. Conscious experience, whether conceptualized in terms of ego, secondary process or sublimation, as viewed by Freudian ego psychologists, or in terms of reclaiming of dissociated affects or relational interactive patterns, as viewed by relational theorists, is stressed over unconscious experience. Unconscious experience becomes merely those meanings that are out of awareness, thereby privileging conscious over unconscious experience. The American relational theorists particularly, in their zeal to discard drive theory, have failed to articulate an accepted conception of the unconscious that is synchronous with relational premises. They are left with an eviscerated version of the unconscious as dissociation, or with a mixed model that uses relational premises to understand and describe the social matrix and more classical drive premises to articulate inner life.

CLASSICAL PSYCHOANALYTIC CONCEPTS OF THE UNCONSCIOUS

The centrality of the unconscious was addressed by Freud (1915) when he stated that the unconscious accounts for gaps in consciousness. In themselves, conscious acts remain disconnected and unintelligible without the link to the unconscious. The unconscious leads us beyond the limits of direct experience, implying that the unconscious is the stuff of symbol and representation, leading us from concrete to more meaningful and creative experiences. "In psychoanalysis there is no choice for us but to assert that mental processes are in themselves unconscious, and to liken the perception of them by means of consciousness to the perception of the external world by means of the sense-organs" (p. 171). What can be perceived and acted upon willfully is derived from those processes that exist on an unconscious level, suggesting a continuous relationship between the perceived and the implicit, between the conscious and the unconscious. Since it is the unconscious that accounts for gaps in consciousness, it is the process of transformation from unconscious to conscious life that is the gap.

There are at least two problems for relational theory with Freud's 1915 conception of the unconscious. First, the spatial metaphors of the topographic theory tend toward a concrete conceptualization of the unconscious and toward a frozen understanding of what is more likely a process than a structure. Gaps in consciousness reflect a process of translation or transformation (e.g., Matte-Blanco, 1975; Civin and Lombardi, 1990), not a place or a static thing occupying space. Second, drive theory led Freud to the notion of the repressed unconscious, and of the unconscious as repressed by definition. According to Freud the system conscious (Cs.) includes the preconscious (Pcs.), or the latent unconscious (Ucs.). The system Ucs. is dynamically repressed, requiring some lifting of the censorship function (through, primarily, excavation of the psychic past) in order to make the transition from the Ucs. to the Pcs. or Cs.

Within the metaphor of energic theory, Freud spoke of the nucleus of the Ucs. as consisting of instincts pressing for discharge. Incompatible or contradictory wishful impulses may exist simultaneously in the Ucs., because there is no censorship or critical function, only contents, cathected with greater or lesser strength. Even within the limitations of drive theory, Freud indicated that the Ucs. is not simply a residue from the process of development, but alive and developing, both influencing and influenced by the Pcs. It is this emphasis on the unconscious as an alive and developing process that finds its way into daily human experience that we wish to articulate here, in a manner consistent with relational psychoanalytic paradigms.

Modern classical critiques of relational theories counterpose the interpersonal or the relational with the intrapsychic and argue that the interpersonal erases the intrapsychic. In contrasting monadic and relational theories of the mind, Wilson (1995) stated, "The mind is not awarded a status in which it merits constructs independent of social relations. . . . The give-and-take of relationship factors is the priority, and the mind disappears from view" (p. 17). Similarly, Murray (1995), in criticizing Aron's (1990) view of transference as a joint creation of patient and analyst, stated, "this position confuses the internal world with the external world, the manifest with the latent" (p. 37).

Both Wilson and Murray bifurcate psychic experience into that which is internal and that which is external. For them this is an essential and fundamental bifurcation, because the internal and the external are made of different stuff. The internal world is composed of instincts, and through development, structures that control instincts, and internal representations that are molded by instincts. The external world, on the other hand, is the world of objective reality. Within this framework, the relational is best explained by the external world, while the self—or, more specifically, those structures of the self that we call the mind—is best explained by reference to the internal world. The premise of their arguments is that relational theory fails to account for the internal psychic life, which they see as essentially instinct driven and nonrelational.

The counter argument that we propose in this work is that drive theory, at least as conceptualized by the American ego psychologists, does not account for the internal life of the mind. Our concept of the unconscious and of its homologue, consciousness, places their origins in relatedness, in primary introjective and projective processes, and not in sexual and aggressive instincts. Unconscious experience retains a dynamic relationship to conscious experience, with each influencing the other in a continuous process.

In drive theory, transformations from unconscious to conscious, when developmentally progressive and not pathological, are linear and unidirectional. The transformations themselves also tend to fit a structural model. A transformation might occur from id into ego, for example, or from action into insight. In our relational view, transformations are bidirectional and dialectic; it is not that the unconscious is made conscious, but that there is a continuous interplay between conscious and unconscious processes, each influencing and transforming the other. Transformative polarities along a relational spectrum might be isolation and communion, for example, or objectivity and subjectivity.

CURRENT RELATIONAL-CONSTRUCTIVIST PROPOSITIONS OF THE UNCONSCIOUS

American relational models can be roughly divided among those in the Sullivanian interpersonalist tradition, those in the self psychological and intersubjective tradition, and those who are influenced by the Kleinian and British Middle School traditions. The interpersonalist tradition is probably the most distinctively American and had a fairly widespread influence on the more orig-

inal and creative contributions of American relational psychoanalysis, particularly modern constructivism. The interpersonalist
view of the unconscious is fundamentally different from the
Freudian view. Harry Stack Sullivan's elaboration of the concept
of unawareness is not equivalent to Freud's concept of the unconscious; one does not stand in for the other (e.g., Zucker, 1989).

For Sullivan (1953), the unconscious depends on the individual social context. Covert processes, which can be understood as
equivalent to unconscious processes, are only apparently private
and insusceptible to the social environment; in origin, they are essentially interpersonal, even those in earliest infancy. The subjective
organization of the self is created from social interactions, and it is
in the context of close examination of social interactions that
change occurs. This position, particularly as it related to the internalization of experience in unconscious life, is reflected in the work
of modern relational theorists such as Stern (1985) and his concept of RIGs (relational interactions that have been generalized),
which form the template of the unconscious organization of experience. Importantly, Sullivan based the development of subjectivity in actual social experience and not in sexual and aggressive
drives. The elaboration of this position by later theorists, however,
has privileged the social context over inner experience, leaving
many who embrace the interpersonal view in the position of
falling back on milder versions of drive defense reductionism to
address inner life. Abrams (1992), for example, resorted to the ego
psychological construct of internal representations to describe the
unconscious, using the static spatial metaphors of structural theory
when he presumably wanted to address unconscious processes.

From a relational-constructivist perspective, which borrows
from the interpersonal tradition, Hirsch and Roth (1995) offer a
contemporary critique of the classical model of the unconscious.
This critique, based on the theoretical differences in the relative
positions of the patient and the analyst with regard to each other,
importantly emphasizes the links between metapsychology and
the clinical attitude. Their critique of the classical model, which
views the unconscious in terms of sexual and aggressive contents
that press for instinctual gratification, takes issue with its archeological view of the patient, with the analyst cast in the role of

excavator of hidden truths and the interpreter of those truths to the patient. They suggest that this view of the unconscious is held by many analysts who consider themselves interpersonal, but who nevertheless resort to classical formulations when considering the unconscious. We very much agree that there are common and un-acknowledged fluctuations between one person and two person psychologies among analysts who consider themselves relational; to us, an insufficiently elaborated view of the related unconscious is at the root of these unacknowledged fluctuations.

A view of the unconscious as the repository of the true self or of buried potential, rather than dynamically repressed, is attributed to what Hirsch and Roth call the developmental arrest model. The developmental arrest model in psychoanalysis most commonly refers back to Kohut (1971, 1977) and the self psychologists and intersubjectivists who followed him (e.g., Stolorow, Brandcraft, and Atwood, 1987). Following Mitchell's (1984) critique of the developmental tilt, the developmental arrest model is viewed as promoting a version of the analyst as benign and parentified, per-forming holding and containing functions with the purpose of nurturing the patient's hidden core of the self. Though this view of the unconscious is quite different from that of classical drive the-ory, Hirsch perceives the clinical attitude as similar in the sense that it excludes the analyst's subjectivity within the analytic dyad. The interpersonal model that Hirsch promotes is that of the uncon-scious as inherently interactive in origin, consisting of unarticu-lated interpersonal experience that is lived out or enacted within the transference/countertransference matrix. From a two-person psychology, the unconscious consists of internalized interpersonal configurations that have been unarticulated and that continue to exert control over the course of one's life. "[T]he articulation of repetitive and internalized patterns of relating and the ultimate ex-pansion of experience" (p. 274) are the goals of the analysis of the unconscious. The unconscious, then, is the material of dissociated relational experience, not of repression of instinctual drive. While consistent with relational or two-person psychology, we under-stand this view of the unconscious as a partial one, perhaps refer-ring more to varying modes of conscious or preconscious being than it does to the unconscious proper.

LANGUAGE, UNCONSCIOUS EXPERIENCE,
AND SOCIAL CONSTRUCTIONISM

Within the Cartesian dichotomy of subjective and objective modes of being, first-person consciousness is an essential attribute of the mind, at the same time that knowledge of the other is radically problematic, experienced as it is through our own subjective states. Cavell (1989a) counterposes Cartesian dualism to a more contemporary constructivist model wherein the phenomenon of meaning is dependent on interactions between minds. In the Cartesian model, thought precedes speech and meaning is mysterious, existing without reference to a material context. In a constructivist model, thought and speech are intertwined and cannot be disembedded from one another. Language is social, not private, rooted in its natural environment and tied to the actions of that environment. In contrasting the Cartesian view that the mind as the locus of meaning is isolated from material objects and other minds, with the constructivist view that meaning is essentially a linguistic phenomenon and language is an interpersonal activity, Cavell (1989b) takes the position that the mind is by definition linguistic and socially embedded. In doing so, she redefines the unconscious.

In finding fault with the Cartesian dualism of Freud's view of the unconscious as timeless and without relation to reality, standing in opposition to consciousness, Cavell posits that unconscious mental structures have the same general features as conscious structures. In both conscious and unconscious realms, thoughts are structured through language. They are meaningfully located in logical space in relation to other thoughts and to a real external world, consisting of beliefs, desires, regrets, intentions, and so on. She argues that a belief or a desire cannot be set entirely free from such considerations of time and place, consistency, or relationship to other beliefs, because it would then be unrecognizable as a belief or a desire. In obliterating notions of timelessness, the relation to reality, and noumena, among others, the unconscious becomes merely dissociated mental contents, governed by the same rules as consciousness.

Concepts of the unconscious and subjectivity are used by Cavell somewhat interchangeably. The development of subjectivity is

posited to occur through relationships to other minds. Internalization, through unconscious identifications of various sorts with
other minds (other objects) creates a multiplicity of minds, in
which Cavell suggests that one mind may function in ways, and to a
degree, like several persons. According to this view, pathology may
be seen in terms of various aspects of the mind that are not on
speaking terms; that is, they have no productive or progressive dialogue arranged with one another. Again, this view limits the unconscious to being that of the container of dissociated experience.

Fourcher (1992) warns against a reductionist tendency in the
constructivist position which, in favoring reflective consciousness,
strips the unconscious of distinctive meaning. He argues against
the position that experience is identified with consciousness, consciousness with linguistic forms, and linguistic consciousness with
knowledge. Reflective consciousness, while a predominant mode
of experience, should not be mistaken for the whole of experience. The constructivists equate the unconscious with nonlinguistic or unformulated experience which is potentially explicable
through language. As such, the unconscious is an implicit form of
the conscious or reflective mind, and not distinctive in itself. All
unconscious experience is expressible through language, leaving
nothing remaining that is inherently unconscious. Implicit is the
notion of an ideal reflective self that is totally conscious, embody-
ing Freud's percept of id becoming ego. The constructivist position embraces the notion of the relative unconscious, while
discarding the absolute or distinctive unconscious. The relative
unconscious may be defined in terms of a relationship between
experience and explicatory statements; that is, as a relationship between nonlinguistic and linguistic modes of experience. This relationship, like Freud's Pcs., is descriptive and nondynamic. In this
system, all experience is either unformulated, or formulated as
conscious, linguistic reflection.

In contrast to the relative unconscious of social constructivism, the absolute unconscious represents the dynamic view,
which "is meant to refer to aspects of experience that are not relative to reflective consciousness. . . . Its value is to codify the formal
otherness of human self-alienation" (p. 324). Fourcher states that
each formulation of the unconscious is incomplete and provides an

inadequate model. "[T]he ideas of a singularly absolute unconscious and its opposite, an exclusively relative unconscious, are necessary only to the extent that the dialectic of social construction and destruction in human experience is thought to be restricted to linguistically structured consciousness" (p. 324–5). This privileging of reflective consciousness, which we believe has its roots in American ego psychology, leaves the constructivists with no framework, with no vocabulary, so to speak, for addressing deep unconscious process. Taking issues with those who revert to the position of the dynamic unconscious when they speak directly of unconscious experience, Fourcher views this problem as reflecting the lack of clarity amongst constructivists about how to characterize deeper levels of interaction that do not involve reflective discourse.

Fourcher points to a political idealism that inheres in constructivist discourse, which he refers to as the idealism of symmetrical relations. Although he uses the terms symmetry and asymmetry in different ways than we shall come to use them in later chapters of this book, his ideas are nonetheless related to ours. The underlying ideal of discourse between reflectively conscious adults is the assumption that experience is symmetrical. In symmetry, one not only experiences what the other experiences, but there is something that is assumed to be equal in the construction; that is, each participant participates equally in constructing the experience of the situation. Humankind has achieved reflective consciousness in necessarily asymmetrical situations; in adult to child interactions, for example, it is not only that the adult has more power than the child, but that the child does not yet share, linguistically, the adult's universe of discourse.

Like Groddeck (1923, 1949), Fourcher suggests that certain experiences consciously appear to be more constructed than constructing, evoking a sense of ourselves as having a momentum or inertia that we can not influence. This sensibility is rooted in early experience and predominates in deeper planes of unconscious experience. Fourcher speaks of these experiences in terms of asymmetry or otherness, whereas we will come to speak of them in terms of symmetry. Nonetheless, we are in agreement that some aspects of immediate, first-person experience remain unavailable to linguistic reflection and must be understood as formally and absolutely distinguishable from consciousness. Unconscious experience is not merely what is momentarily unavailable to the reflective unconscious, but a distinct mode of experience that complements consciousness.

We have reservations similar to Fourcher's about the modern constructivist position's view of the unconscious merely as the formation of relational schemas that remain out of awareness. We see this position as a particular relational twist on the conservative view of the unconscious as the repository of pathological and irrational schemas of the patient's past. It is still an archeological, unipsychic view, though framed within a two-person psychology. We wish to move beyond the concept of the unconscious merely as that which is dynamically repressed or as that which holds dissociated contents, to a concept of the unconscious existing in dynamic relation to conscious processes, serving a linking or translating function between the internal and the external worlds, between self and other, in ways that are the source of intimacy, creativity, and discovery.

Creation and Discovery

Unconscious psychic experience is portrayed by Wolstein (1982) as the movement between creation and discovery: "That is, both to create new experience from the spontaneous, still-unlived possibilities never before envisioned; and to discover old possibilities in conditioned, still forgotten experience already lived through. These two aspects of creation and discovery are co-active and interpenetrating, and they are found to coalesce in the movement of unconscious psychic process and pattern becoming conscious" (p. 413).

The process of discovery is most similar to the repressed or dissociated unconscious, which transforms the once known (or once experienced), yet unacknowledged, to the reknown or recognized. The process of creation, however, is a notion of the unrepressed unconscious, which forms new patterns or new perspectives from preexisting ones, so that what is known is a new actuality, never before experienced. Wilner's (1975) notion of the unrepressed unconscious is that which is present, but yet to be discovered. Extended by the Jungian collective unconscious, which postulates universal human experience that is yet to be individually formulated, and by Platonic universal knowledge, which already exists in the real world but which is awaiting discovery, Wilner implicitly suggests some mode of translation of the apersonal to the personal, and of inner experience to shared experience.

Wilner's emphasis on intimacy, in the whole of human relatedness and especially within the analytic relationship, suggests that intimacy may serve that translating function. In contrast to Freud, with his focus on libidinal and aggressive energies, and Sullivan, with his dismissal of unique individuality, Wilner stresses a perspective of intimacy that maintains that unconscious experience—dissociated, repressed, or otherwise—"represents a potentially intimate aspect of the individual which may be a source for the creation and discovery of new psychic structure and experience, in addition to the repressed area of the unconscious" p. 224). The unconscious is then inherently a relational process. It is through intimacy that the expanding of consciousness occurs, not merely in its dissociative, but also in its creative aspects.

Newirth (1996) advocates a view of the unconscious, within relational theory, which retains its primacy as a developing structure of the mind, encompassing the irrational and the mysterious as a necessary counterforce to the rational and the knowable. This view retains Freud's early focus of the unconscious itself as a source of energy, creativity, and power (more truly a life force), at the same time that it places the unconscious within relational theory at the center of transformations of concrete to symbolic experience. Following the Kleinians, he sees the unconscious as a "developing set of capacities to organize experience in progressively integrated, irrational, and symbolic forms, . . . a developmental . . . rather than a static view of the unconscious as a container for either drive derivatives or childhood relational schemas . . . [that] involves two dimensions: . . . specific categories of experience, such as love and hate or reparation and destructiveness, and . . . levels of symbolic organization, from concrete and fragmented to symbolic and integrated" (p. 9). The capacity to integrate experience is a primary unconscious mode, which Newirth views as involving a dialectic between the paranoid-schizoid and the depressive positions, articulating unconscious experience through two-person structures. These structures move developmentally from concrete interpersonal experiences to symbolic relational phantasies that are expanding sources of power, energy, and creativity. So unconscious experience is not merely made of repetitive internalized relational patterns from childhood, as mainstream relational theory would have it, but in itself functions transformatively.

With acknowledgment to Matte-Blanco (1975, 1988), Newirth's view of the unconscious is not of a static system of physical drives or of repetitive childhood relational schemas, but of a system of mathematical or logical functions that are involved in organizing experience, generating creative experiences of self in the world. In this way, he criticizes mainstream relational theory as having as static and unbalanced a view of the unconscious as drive theorists. In this view, the conscious is not favored over the unconscious, nor is external experience favored over internal experience; rather, the unconscious is a balance or a counterpart of the conscious. One does not subsume, evolve into, or replace the other in linear developmental fashion; rather, the two exist in dialectical relation to one another, each informing the other, transforming and deepening lived experience.

The Unconscious as Infinite Sets: An Experiential Model

We find Matte-Blanco's (1975, 1988) reconceptualization of conscious and unconscious processes to be most salient to relational theory in general, and to our extension of relational theory specifically. Matte-Blanco (1975) described structural theory, introduced in the *Ego and the Id* (Freud, 1923), as having compressed the unconscious of earlier Freud in favor of the elaboration of the ego. The old unconscious was present everywhere as the true psychical reality; the new unconscious is confined to a zone of the mind. Such spatial comparisons are inadequate and, according to Matte-Blanco, need to be replaced with concepts of "intermediate zones," rather than of two or three separate dimensions. The unconscious is not simply a quality, or a structure equivalent to id, but a mode of being. Symmetrical and asymmetrical modes of being are proposed to account for and extend the original Freudian conceptions of the mind in its unconscious and conscious aspects.

Matte-Blanco formulated a systematic investigation of psychical reality in terms of the relationship unconscious-conscious, or symmetrical-asymmetrical. Psychical life is viewed as a perpetual dynamic interaction involving both tension and union between two fundamental types of being that exist within each of us; that which becomes understandable through the principle of symmetry, and that which becomes visible in consciousness and comprehensible through asymmetry. Asymmetry is roughly guided by Aristotelian logic, wherein difference and multiplicity prevail; symmetry is guided by such qualities of the unconscious elaborated by Freud as timelessness, spacelessness, a lack of mutual contradiction, and absence of negation, wherein sameness and unity prevail.

Matte-Blanco applied mathematical set theory to explicate principles of symmetry, whereby the symmetrical unconscious treats the converse of any relation as identical with the relation. That is, it treats asymmetrical relations as if they were symmetrical. For example, John is the father of Peter; Peter is not the father of John, is an example of asymmetrical relations. John is the father of Peter; Peter is the father of John, is an example of symmetrical relations, or, of asymmetrical relations represented as symmetrical in the unconscious. Within this set theory model, dimensions of unconscious life are defined by the relationships among an infinite number of sets or classes.

The symmetrical mode of being has the quality of being unconscious as a constitutive aspect of its nature. The asymmetrical mode of being is experience that is seen or revealed in consciousness and determines the unconscious nature of symmetry. Asymmetry distinguishes and differentiates, which cannot be done through symmetrical relations. As asymmetry cannot encompass the indivisible fullness of symmetry, the asymmetrical realm is limited and confined, and it limits and confines the volume of symmetrical experience that can become conscious.

Symmetrical and asymmetrical modes of being are not equivalent to unconscious and conscious modes; rather, they are incidentally unconscious or conscious. In Matte-Blanco's words, "the quality of being unconscious is not inherent in or essentially inevitable to symmetrical being. It is, instead a consequence of the nature of consciousness, which cannot contain within itself the symmetrical being" (1975, p. 97). And further, "With symmetrical relations alone it is not possible to establish a difference between individual things; hence, the individual is, in this case, identical to the class. Thinking requires asymmetrical relations. So does consciousness. . . . Nothing prevents us, however, from conceiving a form of consciousness which can apprehend an infinite number of things simultaneously. If this were so, symmetrical being would be able to enter consciousness in toto and be apprehended by consciousness . . . for this to be possible, consciousness would have to have infinite dimensions. In this case symmetrical being would be able to enter that infinite-dimensional consciousness. . . . Thinking and being would then come to coincide" (p. 97–8).

Although symmetrization is not equivalent to the unconscious, it is nevertheless most characteristic of the unconscious. Principles of symmetry are incompatible with linear concepts of time, space, and movement. The unconscious, in using symmetrical logic, treats the converse of any relation as identical to it. Thus, it treats asymmetrical relations as symmetrical. Principles of symmetry clearly apply on deep levels of relatedness; for example, the symmetrical statement "My mother loves me; I love my mother" makes good psychic sense and good common sense, as a loved child is a loving one. Similarly, "My analyst is good to me; I am good to (for) him," is an essential symmetrization of the psychoanalytic relationship.

It is important to note that symmetrization is not distortion; it is an essential experience of sameness or identity, a mode of being that is equivalent in status with that of asymmetry. The classical unconscious, the unconscious as the harbor for instincts and repressed psychic contents, is considered, by Matte-Blanco, to be asymmetrical. Instincts and their derivatives necessitate delineation, which is incongruent with symmetry. Deep unconscious experience does not require repression to develop; it is, by nature, symmetrical and unrepressed. Symmetry and asymmetry are linked through a translating or unfolding function, which continuously transforms internal and external experience. This continuous transformation of internal-external experience exists from the beginning of life (even, it is suggested, in utero); it is intrinsic to the human condition. Conflict and motivation do not give rise to or account for these processes, although they may become involved in them.

When stated in object-relational terms, these two fundamental modes of being, the symmetrical and the asymmetrical, correspond to poles of fusion or dedifferentiation (representing unconscious symmetrical relationships) and separateness or differentiation (representing asymmetrical relationships). The symmetrical mode represents the fundamental unity of subject and object within the basic matrix of projection and introjection, whereas the asymmetrical mode represents difference, distinction, and individuality. The asymmetric mode of being provides an impression of multiplicity within a basic homogeneity; as Matte-Blanco said, "symmetry is always wrapped in asymmetry" (1975, p. 113).

As a residue of developmental ego psychology, Matte-Blanco privileges symmetry over asymmetry to the extent that he sees symmetrical being as the basic, the primary, the fundamental state in the individual. Consciousness happens, he stated, whereas symmetrical being is. Asymmetrical relations serve the function of barriers permitting differentiation. "It is the action of the limiting asymmetry preventing the invasion of all generalizing symmetry, which would destroy all structures" (1975, p. 131). According to this framework, the notion of multiplicity of selves (e.g., Mitchell, 1993) would be seen as an illusion of heterogeneity serving to delimit basic experience in the symmetrical or indivisible mode.

Symmetry and asymmetry exist with one another in at least two ways. The first, which Matte-Blanco terms bilogic, is the mixing of asymmetry and symmetry. When the conscious mind expects a bivalently logical (paired) sequence, but symmetrization has been inserted, then there is a bilogical structure. The other, called bimodality, is the coexistence of symmetry and asymmetry, with each simultaneously expressed in the same piece of reality. It is not interpenetration of the one with the other, nor is it cooperation; each, so to speak, ignores the other, expressing only itself. Matte-Blanco re-formulated the Freudian unconscious in terms of bilogic: " . . . the heterogenic mode is the realm of the logical. The symmetrical mode is the realm of illogical. The Freudian mode is the realm of bilogical structures, and, as such, the realm of antinomies" (1988, p. 823).

According to principles of symmetry, at the deepest layers of our minds, we experience a unity; all is one and the same, and there are no distinctions, only identities. Depth and surface of mental activity refer to more inclusive or less inclusive dimensions of psychical life; they do not imply structure or early or late developmental origins. Spatial metaphors are used for convenience and clarity, but the various strata or dimensions of the mind are differentiated conceptually according to the degree of symmetrization. This stratification is governed by bilogic, because thinking requires the presence or perception of some difference or distinction. Symmetrical thinking interpenetrates asymmetrical thinking in greater or lesser degrees, from deeper to more superficial levels. Human experience can be formulated as structures by an infinite series of strata, or dimensions, to use a less spatial metaphor, in which the capacity to recognize differences declines as the amount of symmetrization increases. At the symmetrical limit, or deepest level, is the indivisible mode.

Matte-Blanco set out five strata—although there may be an infinite number—with gradations in each. The first, conscious awareness of separate objects, is best described as delimited, asymmetrical thought. The second contains a significant amount of symmetrization within asymmetrical thinking; bivalent thinking still obtains, but with bilogical structures. The experience of affect and metaphorical thought characterize this level. On the third stratum, different classes are identified, but parts of a class are always taken as the whole. Identifications would apply here, as well as idealization, racism, and prejudice. On the fourth level, wider classes are symmetrized, while some class differentiation remains. The deepest level tends toward mathematical indivisibility—an endless number of things tend mysteriously to become only one thing. In this dimension, thinking is greatly impaired.

Normal individuals are able to feel the continuity between strata, and this capacity or awareness is part of ordinary experi-

ence—it is taken for granted. There are continuous transformations of experience, from unconscious to conscious, from inside
to outside, from self to other, without any break or fracture or
confusion between strata. In abnormal states, this continuity of
differentiation between the strata becomes fractured or confused.
So we know, under normal circumstances in conscious bivalent
logic, that we are not God, for example, at the same time that we
may experience, in the third or fourth stratum, our existence as
godly, or the universe as one.

Matte-Blanco's formulations are consonant with Kleinian theory, but push beyond the spatial metaphors of inside and outside
to which Kleinian theory is wed. Our corporeal existence roots us
in a three-dimensional world; the mind, however, and mathematical set theory to which Matte-Blanco referred, can conceive
of more than three dimensions. Introjective and projective processes, used in the Kleinian senses, are both essential to the development of object relations theory and limit thinking, because they
use three-dimensional spatial metaphors to describe psychical
phenomena in physical corporeal terms. Psychic experience is
framed in space and time even when it is not predominantly
spatio-temporal. The use of the terms modalities and dimensions
was an attempt to describe psychical experience without evoking
spatial, temporal, or archaeological analogy.

Matte-Blanco offered symmetrization to explain projection
and projective identification. He took Klein's (1946) statement:
"Insofar as the mother comes to contain the bad parts of the self
she is not felt to be a separate individual but is felt to be the bad
self" (p. 8) and explicated it as a simultaneously asymmetrical/
symmetrical bilogical structure. Here, two modes of being exist,
one for which reality is divisible and one for which reality is indivisible. Two persons are the same person. Projective identification
is such a bilogical structure, requiring the perception of difference
to then deconstruct boundaries into sameness. Matte-Blanco
stated, "Therefore, the concept of projective identification contains the concept of indivision and also that of distinction; the object and the self are the same *and* are different" (1988, p. 149). He
viewed Klein as writing in bilogic and bimodality and parsed her
according to these systems.

Clinically, the conflicts and anxieties associated with projective identification can be seen in terms of excessive symmetrization, a fear of losing one's own (asymmetrical) identity and being sucked up into indivision, which is felt to be annihilation. On the other hand, these same symmetrical experiences may be simultaneously felt as positive and constructive, not arousing anxiety. Depending upon our experience, we tend to utilize more or less vital bilogical structures. For example, idealization may be a vital symmetrization, leading to experiences of love/beauty, and goodness. Nonvital symmetrization, which Matte-Blanco called symmetrical frenzy, can lead to an experience of destructiveness and interference with thought.

Matte-Blanco conceptualized projective identification in terms of three basic levels of depth. He termed the most superficial level the region of happening, or movement. This level is characterized by the most ample use of asymmetric relations, with the focus on distinctions between subject and object. Both disavowal (this is not mine, you take it) and delegation (this was once mine, please have it) operate here. The deepest level is the region of the basic introjective-projective matrix, where symmetrization prevails. This region is characterized by atemporality and by a lack of distinction between projection and introjection; that is, there is an obliteration of boundaries between inside and outside. The region of intermediate levels of introjection and projection is most characterized by bilogical structures. Asymmetrical relations may prevail at the same time that space-time is dissolving and symmetrical relations begin to intrude. We have developed concepts of subjective and objective identificatory modes of relating, which are defined in the following chapter, to address the deepest symmetrical region of the basic projective-introjective matrix from the subject-relations paradigm.

Matte-Blanco's reconceptualization of unconscious processes, through the development of early (pre–1923) Freudian and later Kleinian ideas, focused on the translating or unfolding function that maps or connects interior or deep unconscious experience with exterior experience. In this system, asymmetrical experience, based on difference, differentiation, and distinction, follows rules of Aristotelian logic. Symmetrical experience, based in sameness, identity, and obliteration of boundaries, follows principles of symmetrization most often associated with unconscious life. These two modes of being coexist and interpenetrate each other, accounting for creativity, vitality, and depth of psychic experience as well as for psychic fracture and confusion.

Although Matte-Blanco did not propose a developmental schema, there are developmental indications that are problematic. These developmental statements skew his theory in the direction of a more conservative ego psychology from which Matte-Blanco has worked so hard to distinguish himself. He stated:

> The deepest strata of the mind . . . are ones where no con-
> flict is experienced. The latter can exist only when opposing
> forces are struggling; something which requires even if on a
> purely symbolic level, both space and time. If infant devel-
> opment is related to the basic matrix, we can see that cur-
> rent views on the ferocity of aggression in the earliest period
> should be modified. Clinical observation reveals that the
> early period may be conflictual only at the superficial levels;
> deep down, they are peaceful. This is, I believe, a more ac-
> curate view of the beginning of life. (1988, p. 195)

This statement seems to us to contradict Matte-Blanco's more clearly articulated position that there is a fundamental antimony of asymmetrical and symmetrical modes of being inherent in human experience. How can human experience, as this statement suggests, originate developmentally in the symmetrical mode, when there is fundamental antinomy? This statement seems to demonstrate Matte-Blanco's difficulty dissembedding himself from the more romantic notions of infancy that inhere in the concept of symbiotic undifferentiation as a primary state. This difficulty leads in the direction of the linear thinking that he worked so hard to avoid.

Using Matte-Blanco's system, we posit that, from the beginning of human experience, the region of the basic identificatory matrix coexists with the region of happening. In earliest life, sensory-motor experience characterizes this region of happening.

Asymmetric (but also symmetric) relations are then articulated through direct contact between sensory-motor experience and the outside world, both animate and inanimate; symmetric (but also asymmetric) relations are articulated through the basic matrix. Even within the basic matrix (presuming that to be a mother-child or other-child matrix), both sameness and difference come to be articulated, so that the symmetrical mode coexists with the asymmetrical mode from the beginning of life. Mental life, then, can be conceptualized in terms of modes and process (rather than structure), characterized from the beginning of life by such elements as transformation and symmetrization, linking functions that are associated with the integration of experience. This conceptualization stands in contrast to the more structural ideas of later Freudian ego psychology and their residue in constructivist relational thought. Mental life is not a structure but, rather, a mode of lived experience and a process of linking between inside and outside, self and other, and symmetric and asymmetric modes of being. It is inherently vibrant, mutative, and subjectively felt.

States of subjectivity are, using Matte-Blanco's terms, governed most by the symmetric mode. Experiences of subjectivity, at least in their origins, involve mutual unconscious relatedness. In subject-relating, two individuals experience their sameness and indivisibility rather than their individuality. They come to feel, at least momentarily, their mutual identification and intimate embeddedness with one another as subjects relating. By contrast, object-relating is governed by the asymmetric mode. In object-relating, individuals come together from positions of psychic separateness to feel bonded and connected, perhaps, but not mutually embedded. The transformations between states of subject relatedness and states of object relatedness integrate psychical experience.

Most commonly in psychoanalysis, the term object relations has been used to refer to unconscious relational experience, describing objectification. We use the term subject relations and related unconscious to describe subjectification in unconscious relational experience and the transformations between subjective and objective experience. These terms are used to distinguish more from less integrated experiences in the symmetric mode, to stress experiences of subjectivity that develop through introjection, and to emphasize the experiential, infinitely dimensional, dialectical and shared nature of psychic life in deeper unconscious dimensions. Psychical experience, from a subject-relational standpoint, is inherently relational, identificatory, and synergistic, grounded in the unconscious dialectical interchange between experience that is shared and subjective and that which is more individuated and objective.

Subject relations theory is distinguished from other notions of relational unconscious processes (e.g., Gerson, 1995) by its emphases on the symmetrical context from which psychic life emerges (and the inherent wholeness in unconscious relatedness that this context brings forth), and by the resurrection of the unconscious as enlivened, vitalizing, and transformative. These qualities contrast with the usual presentation of the unconscious as an inorganic structure composed of repressed/dissociated contents, and the usual emphases on the separateness of unconscious minds and subjectivities and/or the individual roots of dyadic reciprocity and relatedness. In the paradigm of subject relations, both subjective and objective unconscious experience develops from a psychical realm in which symmetrical unity and subject-relating reign. This is the realm of the related unconscious.

2

DIALOGUES OF THE UNCONSCIOUS

Naomi Rucker and Karen Lombardi

The idea that the unconscious is shared, is shareable, and is mutually constructed or cocreated in both the original developmental relationship and in the psychoanalytic field is traceable directly to Ferenczi (1915). Wolstein (1993) credited Ferenczi with making the first serious approach to formulating the shared nature of the patient-analyst relationship in its conscious and unconscious aspects. Ferenczi wrote of unconscious dialogues "where, namely, the unconscious of two people completely understand themselves and each other, without the remotest conception of this on the part of the consciousness of the other" (p. 109). Ferenczi's ideas of mutual analysis and active technique are experiments or offshoots of the idea that the unconscious of individuals are in dialogue with one another and that they co-create experience.

The unconscious dialogues through which experience is mutually created are not readily appreciated through conventional notions of unconscious and conscious process or the linear logic that characterizes psychoanalytic explanations in the main. Many phenomena that reflect this dialogical process are misconstrued as irrelevant to psychoanalytic inquiry and ignored because they are not explicable through linear thinking. Such phenomena develop from within the symmetrical (Matte-Blanco) or symbiotic (Searles) milieu in which patient and analyst are subjectively immersed and in which subjective experience becomes shareable. They represent the bidirectional unconscious communication and mutual identifying processes that occur in the context of experiences of dedifferentiation. They are not apprehendable via the conscious rationality upon which usual psychoanalytic notions rest.

Correspondences are one class of unconsciously communicated phenomena that emerge from within this shared unconscious space. Occurrences such as parallel dreams and the unconscious catch, which are described in subsequent chapters of this book, are striking manifestations of correspondent phenomena and unconscious communication within the psychoanalytic realm. In less dramatic forms in and outside of the consulting room, themes of intuition, certain transference/countertransference phenomena, and prescient knowledge also fit into this category. Among relational phenomena, correspondences are prime illustrations of the unconscious dialogues that frame subject relations. The following are two brief examples of unconscious communication occurring in the form of psychical correspondences.

CLINICAL EXAMPLES

Chris

Chris, a young adult patient who saw her analyst primarily as a mother figure, and towards whom she felt possessive, dreamt for years of "Elena." Her thoughts led to an Elena in her high-school class about whom she had some feelings and associations, but not of an intensity to warrant repeated dreams. She was always perplexed by the repeated occurrences of Elena in her dream life over the years of her analysis. During her termination session, she asked her analyst if she had any children and her analyst replied, "Yes, a son Mark and a daughter Elena."

Michelle and Martha

Two colleagues were discussing a patient of one of them over lunch. Michelle, the therapist, was describing her difficulty feeling comfortable with a patient she had been seeing for a number of months. The patient, Martha, was a nun who seemed positively inclined towards Michelle and with whom the work had been progressing. However, Michelle was feeling increasingly uncomfortable in Martha's presence for reasons she could not define. While they were talking, Michelle's colleague was playing with the table cloth and at one point said, "Look at this design. It looks like a Swastika!" Michelle's eyes widened and she responded, "I didn't want to say this—I feel like it is a terrible accusation—but I sense that Martha is anti-Semitic and that's why I'm not comfortable. I was working up to admitting it to you."

Mutual Subjectivity and the Uncanny

These types of unconscious phenomena are often described as uncanny, a word that is particularly rich for this context. Freud (1919) saw things uncanny as "that class of the frightening which leads back to what is known of old and long familiar" (p. 220). It is the return of something familiar to the individual—or to humans collectively—that has been removed from consciousness. To Freud, the reemergence of repressed desire evokes an unsettling feeling because the repressed material is no longer recognized consciously. In our thinking, however, this material may be recognized unconsciously as familiar, but disowned, and the clashes between unconscious recognition, disavowal, and conscious nonrecognition generate the sense of the uncanny.

In English, the root word "canny," means shrewd; thus, uncanny refers to something that is not shrewd, or something that is straightforward and overt. Within the context of unconscious communication, things that are uncanny, paradoxically, often are deceptive; it is their "canniness" that makes them uncanny. In German, as Freud (1919) points out, the word for uncanny is *unheimlich*. The root word "*heimlich*" has a twofold meaning, referring to both "familiar, intimate, belonging to the home," and to "secret, or hidden" (p. 222); thus, *unheimlich* would appear to be the opposite of familiar or hidden. Customarily, however, *unheimlich* is used only as contrary to the first meaning of *heimlich*, that of being familiar, not in respect to the second, that of being secret. Thus, things that are *unheimlich* (uncanny) are things that are expected to be kept out of sight, but which have come to light; they are things that are secretly known, yet also unfamiliar.

Uncanny and *heimlich*, then, are words that enfold on their opposite. In containing antithetical meanings, they illustrate the condensation, homogeneity, and multidimensionality that characterize both the symmetrical mode of being and subject relations. The latent meanings and valences of these words also mirror the essence of unconscious communication and correspondent phenomena, which both reveal concealed (dissociated) experience and reflect close psychic ties. In contrast to Freud, who saw the "return of the repressed" in the uncanny as the surfacing of unconscious intrapsychic desires, we see correspondent phenomena as expressions of the related unconscious. Their roots lie in the infinite layers of a dyadic relationship and in the wellspring of creative energy and enlivenment that exists within the related unconscious. Uncanny correspondences exemplify Newirth's (1996) understanding of things irrational and mysterious as a necessary counterbalance to those things rational and knowable.

While the term unconscious communication at first seems to offer a satisfactory nomenclature for such correspondent phenomena, upon closer examination it is a term that carries with it the assumption of psychical differentiation that is ill suited for this context. The nomenclature of unconscious communication describes two individuals communicating to each other unconsciously. It does not embody the concept of unitary, symmetrical experience wherein self and other, subject and object are indistinguishable, nor does it convey the fundamental knowing of the other that is present in subject relations. Things must be communicated only if they are not immediately and fundamentally known. Unconscious communication is appropriate terminology if one is discussing correspondent phenomena solely from an asymmetrical vantage point, but it is otherwise a term with limited richness and application. It is more meaningful to speak of correspondent phenomena as representing the immersion in mutual subjectivity, an unconscious experience not reliant on communication as communication is usually comprehended.

Explanatory Frameworks

The positivistic assumptions carried by the term unconscious communication nevertheless have been central to traditional explanations of correspondent phenomena, of which there have been few. As an alternative framework to traditional conceptualizations, a general continuum of ideas is presented here, along which psychical correspondences can be explained. This spectrum includes positivistic assumptions, but is not confined to them. The chosen theories represent diverse positions and either directly, or with minimal extrapolation, offer insights into unconsciously communicated phenomena.

Points along this explanatory continuum represent degrees of assumptions of psychic separateness with asymmetrical logic and subject-object differentiation at one pole and symmetrical logic and subject-object undifferentiation at the other. Analytic meaningfulness also can be described along this spectrum in inverse relation to gradations in separateness. Analytic meaningfulness expands as the theoretical models incorporate psychical unity in their understandings. Thus, the most common explanations, those most reliant on psychic separation, are the least meaningful within an analytic context and are most removed from analytic principles. The more fruitful, and the most analytically congruent, explanations derive from paradigms that allow for multidimensional meaning and that are not constrained by positivistic principles.

At the end of our continuum most consistent with asymmetrical logic and psychic discreteness are the positivistic explanations discussed by Eisenbud (1970). In one of the few writings on the topic of unconscious communication, Eisenbud offered three standard hypotheses to account for correspondences between two people's dreams: 1) coincidence; that is, a chance occurrence; 2) the dreamers were, independently or not, subject to similarly acting influences; 3) there was some kind of (conscious) communication between the dreamers that was responsible for the correspondence. Eisenbud concludes that there is no typical manifest content in dreams and infers that correspondences in content are not random events, but have meaning. Eisenbud then developed an explanation for correspondences based upon extrasensory perception.

While these hypotheses provide intellectually acceptable explanations, they have the weakest, least meaningful explanatory power and are farthest removed from analytic theory. They do not provide room for the exploration of unconscious meaning and, as a consequence, they have contributed to the dismissal of many correspondent occurrences from analytic examination. In bringing analytic attention to such phenomena through descriptions of his own correspondent experiences as an analyst, Eisenbud considered a kind of ESP or telepathy as a likely explanatory framework. In doing so, he went far outside of usual scientific or analytic paradigms to ascribe analytic meaning to these experiences. It is possible to examine correspondences through analytic postulations (although not through traditional analytic understandings); such an approach is preferable in amplifying the analytic significance of psychical correspondent phenomena.

Bollas (1992) wrote specifically on unconscious communication using both ego-psychological and object-relational models. He described the task of attempting to decipher latent meaning in the patient's communications while listening to the patient's text. The analyst tracks the patient's unconscious through a kind of deconstructive capacity in order to break down conscious communication into its unconscious components following, for example, defensive maneuvers, condensations, and so on. Bollas viewed this process as facilitated by the analyst's unconscious, by his capacity to free-associate or to dream in relation to the patient, which renders him more receptive to the patient's unconscious communications. Although Bollas' model has analytic significance, it remains

rooted in a two-person orientation in which each party is psychically differentiated from the other. Consequently, this model is
based upon asymmetrical patterns and must attempt to fit unconsciously communicated phenomena into an asymmetrical framework for which they are poorly suited.

From a point on our continuum that is also analytically meaningful (but less asymmetrical), one can construct an explication of
correspondences using Racker's (1968) object-relational postulations of concordant and complementary identifications. Through
concordance and complementarity, patient and analyst express their
identity with each other. Racker's focus is on mutuality and activity
in the psychoanalytic relationship, as opposed to passive and au-
thoritarian postures. Mutuality and activity function through momentary shifts in consciousness and unconsciouness within the
transference-countertransference relationship. Racker's thinking allows for ideas of unconscious mutuality, but his constructs of concordance and complementarity reflect the asymmetrical premise
of psychic separateness that distinguishes object-relational from
subject-relational thought.

In concordant identifications, each part or structure of the analyst's personality is identified with the corresponding part or structure in the patient; the analyst's ego or superego is allied with the
patient's ego or superego, the analyst's id with the patient's id. In
complementary identifications, the analyst's personality structures
exist in complementary opposition to—rather than in correspondence to—the patient's personality. In both forms of identification,
the analyst perceives the patient's basic object representational configuration, and makes contact with the patient's internal reality
through countertransference. The relational experience thus created
essentially constitutes a repetition compulsion, wherein the new situation repeats original patterns of identification and relatedness.

Concordance and complementarity develop separate modes of
relatedness. Concordance is embedded in homogeneity, establishing a unity or identity between the two participants. It calls forth
the experience of attunement or empathic connection in a positive
mode. Complementarity exists along heterogeneous—rather than
homologous—lines, generating disidentification and evoking experiences of difference or alienation. In Racker's (1968) words,

concordant identifications are founded upon "a resonance of the exterior within the interior, a recognition of what belongs to another
as one's own ('this part of you is I') and on the equation of what is
one's own with what belongs to another ('this part of me is you')"
(p. 134). From a Kleinian perspective, concordance is lived in the
depressive position in which identifications are based on incorporation, whereas complementarity is lived in the paranoid-schizoid
position in which identifications are based on disavowal. The more
dissociated certain affects are for the analyst and/or patient, and the
more toxic certain internal objects are, the harder it is to carry out
concordant identifications, and the more likely it is for one to remain mired in complementary situations.

Although concordance and complementarity stem from an object-relations model, they can be expressed in terms of identificatory modes of relatedness, placing them within a subject-relational
frame of reference. Within an object-relational paradigm, concordance refers to a process of introjection, through which parts of
the other are experienced as existing within the self, whereas complementarity refers to projection, through which parts of the self
are experienced as existing in the other. Both projection and introjection assume psychic boundaries and are based on bifurcation, or
splitting. Within a subject-relational paradigm, introjection corresponds to a subjective identificatory mode of relating, wherein the
other is identified as self, and projection corresponds to objective
identificatory mode of relating, wherein is the other is identified as
not-self.

In these modes of identification, boundaries are absent (subjective mode) or minimal (objective mode). Self and other are differentiated by the extraction from wholistic symmetrical experience of
aspects of that wholism that come to be felt as residing in and
belonging to the self, or felt as residing in and belonging to the
other as not-self. Symmetrical experience is divided or cleaved—
rather than bifurcated—by this extraction. Implicit in the word
cleave are the dual meanings of division and adherence that connote
a concurrent separation from and bond with the symmetrical stratum. While otherness is identified as not-self in surface dimensions
of unconscious experience, in deep unconscious dimensions other
and self share a common genesis and are experienced as the same.

The cleavage into self and non-self identifications leaves behind un-differentiated, and unpotentiated, experience that continues to oc-cupy, and define, the region of the related unconscious.

We have borrowed the concept of modes from Matte-Blanco to express the experiential states of identification that exist in the related unconscious realm. Although Matte-Blanco (1988) dis-cusses a symmetrical layer of projective-introjective identification, in which boundaries are obliterated and projection and introjec-tion are indistinguishable, the terms projective and introjective identification more commonly designate asymmetrical identifica-tions, such as those depicted by object-relations theory. The term subjective identificatory mode of relatedness signifies identifica-tion within symmetrical experience, whereas the term objective identificatory mode of relatedness addresses identification origi-nating at the boundary between symmetry and asymmetry where self-other differentiation first emerges.

This nomenclature favors the experiential and relational quali-ties of identification over content or process and refers implicitly to related unconscious experience. The idea of identification as con-tent or process, which implies psychic differentiation, linear time, and progressive movement, is exchanged for the idea of mode, which deemphasizes psychic differentiation to imply timeless expe-rience and dialectical interchange. The formal definition of mode, a manifestation of an underlying substance, is suited to the infinite dimensionality that is critical to subject-relational thought.

The term identificatory modes of relating is preferred over the simpler word identification because identification denotes a fixed event or thing, rather than fluidity of experience. This term is con-sistent with the dialectical interplay of self and other, subjectivity and objectivity, symmetry and asymmetry that is central to subject relations postulations. Since subject-relations theory considers identification and relatedness to be intrinsic to psychical experi-ence, the abbreviated phraseology, subjective or objective modes may be appropriate when a subject-relational context is unequivo-cally clear. The terms relational modes or identificatory modes also may be used for brevity under more equivocal conditions. Concordance and complementarity, thus, are construed, from a subject-relational framework, as different processes of identifica-

tion corresponding, respectively, to a subjective or objective identificatory mode of relating (or to a subjective or objective relational or identificatory mode).

Although Racker's object-relational model maintains distinctions between self and other, interior and exterior, it also permits
shared unconscious experience and incorporates an understanding that the relationships between self and other, subject and object, projection and introjection fluctuate. His model stands at the
border between more symmetric and more asymmetric expositions germane to correspondent phenomena. Like symmetry and
asymmetry, object-relating and subject-relating can coexist on different planes of psychic life. Through basic projective and introjective identificatory situations and the transformations between
them that unconsciously communicate experience and through
which unconscious experience is shared, relational contact is
made, and correspondent phenomena are created.

An alternative model of correspondences that represents a
point on the explanatory continuum closer to symmetry was offered by Wilner (1991) in his concept of communion. In Wilner's
view, communal experience may be a carryover from mother-
child communication patterns of early infancy that are obscured,
but not eradicated, by subsequent cognitive development. In
communion, two individuals in participation with each other are,
precisely because of their participation, part of a common psychological context. In this context, unlike in the perceived external
world, things are organized according to underlying common
psychological constellations or centers and not in temporal, linear
order. Communion relies upon the transmission of experience
without the necessity of conscious thought, formative action, or
psychic separation. Experience that is present is absorbed without
conscious or behavioral mediation. In this way, the term communion is a more encompassing and less limiting language than unconscious communication. The concept of communion serves as
a link between other theories of unconscious communication and
the larger constructs of symmetry and subjective relatedness.

Searles' (1979) discussion of the mutual immersion of patient
and analyst in symbiotic relatedness also reflects the idea of a shared
unconscious context in which the boundaries of self-definition give

way to mutual subjective experience. In Searles' words, "The very fact of one's preoccupation with the uniqueness of one's own identity is likely to be serving as a defense against one's unconscious fear of recognizing that human existence is lived largely at a symbiotic level of relatedness" (p. 503). Searles asserts that there are times in psychoanalysis when it is impossible to "maintain a clear differentiation between the patient's illness and the analyst's own self, to such a degree that he feels on occasion fully and directly—not merely partially and vicariously—reponsible for the patient's illness, by reason of his subjective experience that he personally *is* that illness" (p. 524). The analyst's subjectivity comes to be involved with the patient's subjectivity, and unconscious identifications that facilitate integration are generated.

Correspondent phenomena, from a subject-relations perspective, call upon the subjective identificatory mode and the mutuality of psychical experience that are echoed in this type of symmetrical relation. Correspondences and like forms of unconscious communication are rooted in the related unconscious realm where mutual subjective experience is omnipresent. Reverberations of mutual subjectivity are integrated and brought to awareness through transformations from unconsciousness to consciousness, symmetry to asymmetry, interior to exterior, and self to other that constitute the dialogues of the related unconscious.

The Unconscious Surround in Related Unconscious Experience

The notion of *surround* conveys the idea that unconscious experience encompasses the individual, in contrast to the conventional idea that unconscious experience is contained within the individual. From this vantage point, correspondences represent the emergence of symmetrical being into the asymmetrical realm of experience. They provide windows onto the deepest dimensions of psychical life where psychological differentiation does not exist. Correspondences require language in order to be reconstructed and communicated at the asymmetrical level, but they are created and lived at the symmetrical level. In this lived quality, they epitomize the creative vitality and mutuality of subject-relating.

From a field that has been called a distant cousin to relational psychoanalysis (Wilner, 1996b), quantum physics, an idea similar to symmetry and germane to subject relations has been produced by Bohm (1980). Bohm's theory rests upon the premise of "unbroken wholeness," which he believes to be a universal property of nature, inherent in cosmic processes at a deep, nonmanifest level. His ideas, independently derived, are akin to Matte-Blanco's speculation of infinite dimensionality and to the ultimate conjunction of symmetrical and asymmetrical modes of being. Bohm called this universal feature of nature "implicate" or "enfolded," constructed in such a way that each part subsumes the whole. An essential feature of this universal implicate order is the existence of consciousness throughout the cosmos. Bohm conceived of mind and matter as interdependent and correlative, but not causally connected as does positivistic science. Mind and matter are mutually enfolding projections of an overarching dimension that is neither mind nor matter.

The essence of Bohm's ideas was experimentally demonstrated in a well-known experiment (Capra, 1982). Two particles were shot into different areas of space from a state of zero spin; that is, they were spinning in opposite directions. They were then directed to drift apart over huge distances and, when they reached a great separation in space, the spin of one particle was measured. Instantaneously, the second particle was observed to spin in corollary fashion to the first, even though there had been no information transfer between them. The two particles were hypothesized to be part of the same context even though they simultaneously continued to exist in separate spheres in the objective world.

In the psychical realm, this notion of a universal context is addressed by constructs of symmetry, communion, and subject relatedness. Unconscious correspondences are an experiential path along which implicate psychical substrates and unconscious dialogues can be made known, just as anaclitic logic is thought to form linguistic pathways from symmetry to asymmetry, and cosmic consciousness in physics is hypothesized to link disparate physical elements. The communal context in which two people in a dyad find themselves is lived, not observed or even participated in. People may participate with each other (an objective position), and they may recognize an unconscious correspondent experience when it occurs (an intermediate position), but they live, psychically, within their subjective immersion with each other (a subjective position).

Unconsciously, individuals know each other from the inside out; consciously, they come to know each other from the outside in. Instances of unconscious communication convey mutual unconscious subjectivity and bring to individual awareness glimpses of the nature, content, and dialogues of the related unconscious. Understanding unconsciously communicated phenomena from other than a positivistic viewpoint requires that notions of direct causality or linearity be put aside, that spatial and temporal considerations and objectivity be disregarded, and that unconscious interrelatedness be considered fundamental and intrinsic to the phenomena. We share with Wilner (1996a) the conviction that feeling engaged in unconscious experience rests more on faith and inspiration, than on rationality and realistic perception. As Wilner brings to our attention, faith and inspiration must come to us, we cannot consciously find them. We can only prevent ourselves from turning away from them through logic and reason when they first appear.

Unconscious experience becomes shareable and shared, and the cocreation of a related unconscious and its dialogues becomes evident, when individual subjectivities give way to mutual subjective experience and two persons fall into things with each other. "Falling into" captures the feeling of suddenly finding oneself intermingled with another in something unexpected, inexplicable, or uncanny that is larger and more encompassing than them. The things into which they fall feel both familiar and disconcerting, and the sense that they have fallen into it is unsettling. They have been *un-settled* by something that they cannot grasp. They cannot grasp (understand) the extraordinary and they cannot grasp (hold) onto the ordinary. In the midst of mutual subjectivity, both participants fall into the dimension of symmetrical experience and into one another, each losing one's self in order to find the familiar and the lost.

3

SOUNDS OF SILENCE
PARALLEL DREAMING AND THE MUTUAL DREAM

Karen Lombardi and Naomi Rucker*

Traditionally, the psychoanalytic process has focused on words, language, and the symbolic meaning of the language employed by the patient within the analytic relationship. In a productive analysis, the patient produces verbal associative material that leads to deeper understanding of his own past life, as well as life as he lives it in transferential relation to the analyst in the present. "Primitive" communication, in contrast, may be verbal or nonverbal, but is thought to derive primarily from developmentally early relational

---

*Clinical material contributed by Naomi Rucker.

experiences that occurred before the acquisition of verbal communication. These early relational experiences, particularly when they take the form of psychic traumata (such as the early death of a parent, having a depressed or psychotic parent, or a childhood illness of notable duration or severity), become solidified or concretized in ways that make them inaccessible through the usual verbal-symbolic codes of free association and discourse with the analyst.

By the term primitive communication, a concept which subsumes the phenomenon of parallel dreaming, such authors as McDougall (1978) mean straying from the usual and expected therapeutic collaboration based on free association and verbal interpretation, and employing some other, less verbal and more affective means of communication. Primitive communication may be accomplished either through silence or through compulsive talking, both of which can serve to keep the analyst at a distance. The function of this distantiation, however, is not to defend the individual from unacceptable thoughts, feelings or impulses, but rather to recreate the breakdown in communication that the patient experienced originally in early relationship to the mother. Within the analytic space, silence may not then indicate resistance to the emergence of conflictual verbal material but rather constitute, in itself, a therapeutic milieu wherein a more basic exchange between patient and analyst may occur.

Although we are in accord with McDougall's description of nonverbal communication as analytically meaningful, we disagree with her use of the term "primitive communication" to refer to developmentally early object-relational experiences, which have not yet been symbolized through the convention of language. We see primitive communication as unformulated unconscious experiences that still struggle to occupy the shared space between analyst and patient. Although they may not be linguistically coded, such experiences are not necessarily developmentally early. Primitive communication is not solely a feature of preoedipal patients who are thought to suffer the developmental arrests of narcissistic or borderline disorders, but rather are an aspect of ordinary human experience at deeper psychic levels.

This chapter presents an instance of primitive communication between patient and analyst that first took place through the medium of silence and then through the medium of the mutual—or shared—dream. The parallel dreaming process that this clinical material illustrates will be examined initially using object-relations principles and then in light of the model of subject relations, which rests on concepts of symmetry, asymmetry, and unconscious context. While object-relations principles can provide an account for primitive communication, such as parallel dreaming, their roots in the essential separateness of individual psyches constrict an appreciation of the analytic meaningfulness of such phenomena.

Lynn and the Shared Dream

Lynn was an educated professional woman in her late thirties who came into analysis during a period of conflict and stress in her relationship with a man. Having been divorced, she was raising her small child alone. She had been involved seriously with a man for a few years, but the relationship suffered increasing difficulties around the issue of a permanent commitment. At the time she began analysis, Lynn was moderately depressed, but functioning well at work and in her relationship with her child. She was physically attractive, personable, and poised in her manner.

Initially, Lynn was able to speak rather freely about her life circumstances and about her anxiety and anger toward the man with whom she was involved. At the same time, she expressed transferential concerns about being criticized and rejected. Early in the analytic work, she made the transition from face-to-face contact to the couch with relative ease. In the second year of analysis, Lynn began to be increasingly silent and to show great difficulty associating freely. She would respond only perfunctorily to the analyst's questions or observations regarding her silence. Although she could be prompted to speak by such interventions, she was not stimulated to produce further verbal associative material.

Lynn described feeling withdrawn, distant, worried that the analyst would be angry and frustrated with her for being silent, and expressed feelings of hopelessness about her therapeutic work. The analyst's suggestion that Lynn already might perceive that her analyst was angry with her was met with denial and further emotional retreat. At other times, however, Lynn also felt comfortable with the silence, a feeling that pointed to its syntonic nature for her. Essentially, she seemed unable to sustain a connection with her analyst through language. During these periods of silence, the analyst felt disconnected and, at times, frustrated. Occasionally, she shared Lynn's sense of hopelessness, feeling defeated at every attempt to engage Lynn. It was not unusual for thirty minutes to pass without any spontaneous verbalization on Lynn's part. A number of sessions passed in total silence except for greeting and leave-taking, which increased the analyst's feelings of breakdown in the analytic relationship.

At this juncture in the analysis, following a few consecutive silent sessions, the analyst had the following dream:

> Lynn and I are in my house, although the house is not ex-actly as it appears in reality. Lynn collapses (faints). I go over to her and, say "Linda, Linda, get up." There is no response. I wonder why I am calling her Linda when her name is Lynn. I dial 911, but there is a tape saying that the number is dis-connected. I am getting more anxious and feel that I cannot help. I go into the living room to look for help, where there are carpet cleaners (men) cleaning the carpet, putting lots of green foam on the carpet. I ask why they are doing that. They respond, "It'll come clean." As I leave the room, I look out of the window and see Lynn's mother sitting in a parked car. I suddenly realize that she and the carpet men are try-ing to kill Lynn and me with the poisonous green foam they are using on the carpet and we have to get out. I feel lots of anxiety in this dream.

The analyst experienced this dream as an expression of the analytic relationship and that same day took the opportunity to discuss it with a colleague. After some consideration, she de-cided to describe the dream to Lynn at their next session, which was scheduled for later that afternoon. When Lynn arrived for her appointment, the analyst expected to wait a few moments to see whether Lynn brought in spontaneous material, and then to attempt to link her own dream with the content of Lynn's asso-ciation. With this in mind, the analyst was much surprised when

Lynn opened the session describing her own dream of the previous night—a dream similar, and at some points identical, to the analyst's dream in manifest content. Lynn's dream follows:

> I am in my old house. It is familiar, but not quite exactly that house. Inside, the house is covered in lush greenery, giving it a Hawaiian atmosphere. Somebody is trying to kill me, but I don't know who. I am feeling anxious, and run into different rooms looking for help. I want to find you, but there is no one there, the rooms are empty. I call 911, but cannot get through. I feel I know who is coming after me, but I cannot remember who it is. I know I have to get out of the house, but I cannot find my way, I feel lots of anxiety.

The analyst listened to the dream, asked a few questions about Lynn's association to particular dream elements, and then said, "I had virtually the same dream last night." Lynn was silent, then giggled nervously, asking, "What do you mean?" The analyst elaborated that she also had a dream in which someone was trying to kill her (Lynn), that there was no help, and the feeling was one of anxiety. Lynn said, "This is like ESP; it's creepy." The analyst responded that it seemed that they were communicating despite the absence of words, like in ESP. Lynn stated that she was feeling nervous, but also was comforted that the analyst "could understand all this." Lynn was then asked whether she had any thoughts about the analyst's dream. The work in this and following sessions led to an articulation of Lynn's rage at her father as a partial displacement of feelings towards her mother, and an appreciation of the disavowal of rage in the analytic dyad. The silence came to be understood as a manifestation of the deadened, lifeless quality of some of her early experiences with her mother that Lynn was unable to communicate verbally, but which were communicated affectively through silence.

Sharing the parallel dreams as a part of the analysis led to an understanding of dissociated rage in both patient and analyst. The dreams represented and served to facilitate identifications between analyst and analysand that allowed that rage to become integrated into the therapeutic relationship and the self. Over the subsequent months, Lynn became dramatically more able to speak freely during sessions, and the chronic sense of futility that she had experienced lifted.

Discussion of the Dreams

The primary elements in both dreams are the setting of a house that is similar to but not identical with reality, the futile search for help that included calling the emergency number 911, the sense of impending murder, and the green coloration. Lynn's description of the house as old can be understood as a reference to her past and as a description of the sense of depressive weariness that she had been experiencing in the analysis. The analyst's creation of the house as her own can be seen as a symbol for the immediate clinical process itself, through which the unconscious experiences of Lynn and her analyst emerged in each others' dream life.

The mutual search for help is a fairly explicit reference to the attempts by both analyst and analysand to feel connected and to mobilize a process that was feeling stagnant. The emergency call to 911 reflected the desperation that both were feeling and not openly expressing. The feeling that the treatment was in a critical state and escape to safety must be found was conveyed through the sense of impending murder and the urgency to get out that both parties felt. Lastly, the green coloration in the carpet foam and the lush greenery likely referred to the green couch and chair in the analyst's office, yet they also contained a polarized expression of the positive and negative qualities in the transference. In the analyst's dream, the green foam that purported to be cleansing (the treatment that heals) is in fact poisonous, reflecting an unconscious experience that seems to reflect persecutory anxiety in the analytic relationship. In contrast, the patient's dream communicates a sense of the therapeutic environment as potentially nurturing, albeit somewhat foreign or exotic. It would seem as if the analyst was, in part, harboring rage and aggression that Lynn sensed and feared was destructive. From an object-relations perspective, it might be said that the analyst served as a repository for such aggressive feelings and impulses, helping to preserve the patient's good experience of the analytic ambiance. At the same time, the split-off rage they both shared was sometimes felt by the analyst to threaten the ongoing alliance and the viability of the analysis. From a subject-relational perspective, the patient, the analyst, and the analysis as targets of destruction as well as potential rescuers, explicate their interpenetrating identities.

Another symbol of the threat that was expressed in the dream can be found in the analysts' misrepresentation of the patient as Linda. The analyst's association to this name was the classical analysis of a colleague named Linda, whose aloof and often unresponsive analyst misunderstood her in a way that ultimately destroyed that analysis. Lynn's analyst, who does not work classically, nevertheless found herself participating in this analysis as a silent partner within a mutually created aloof atmosphere. The analysis was proceeding in a more formally correct and ordinary way, different than the way in which this analyst typically worked. The dream carries with it the recognition that the patient, by being called the wrong name, is somehow being misrepresented in the analysis.

Paradoxically, contained in the recognition that something was wrong was also contained the knowledge that something is right; in the dream Lynn is called a fuller, more formal version of her name, a name which contains her real name. The Lynn that needed to be contacted was contained within the Linda whom the analyst was addressing. Similarly, deeper levels of communication and identification were contained within the silence and frustration. Lynn was in danger of being lost within herself and within the analyst's conscious sense of who she was. In calling her by the wrong name, the analyst brought into the foreground the need to find the lost core of Lynn.

Winnicott (1963) provides one framework for understanding such clinical phenomena in his discussion of communicating and not communicating. He postulates that active noncommunication (as in silence) may be understood in terms of making room for a sharing between the patient's true-self and the analyst. Ordinary communication may be compliant talk, linked with some degree of false self object-relating. Active noncommunication, then, may serve to protect the real self as well as the relationship with the real-self analyst. Within the symbolism of the analyst's dream, the real-self (Lynn) was disguised within the false-self, the formally correct, compliant Linda.

The element that most clearly discriminates between the patient's and the analyst's dream is the identification of Lynn's mother as a potential murderer. From an object-relations base, it could be interpreted that the analyst unconsciously had absorbed the patient's destructive maternal introjects, which she recognized on a subliminal level, while the patient could feel only the anxiety that surrounded them. From a subject-relations viewpoint, the analyst came to *be* the patient, that is, to be the one with the threatening mother. Both the misnaming of Lynn in the analyst's dream and the analyst's confusion about it can be understood to represent this shift in the locus of subjectivity. Neither person was quite the person that she objectively appeared to be. In the analyst's dream, the mother is outside the house, that is, outside the analyst's consciousness. Lynn's mother existed apart from the analysis, not fully integrated within the analyst's self, but connected to the carpet men (symbolically, the patient's father, who frequently "called her on the carpet"). The inability of either Lynn or the analyst to articulate consciously and verbally the rage and aggression associated with Lynn's inner sense of her relationship with her mother was perceived unconsciously as an immediate and lethal threat to the integrity of the analysis. Both the absence of conscious articulation and the mortal threat imposed by the dissociated rage were expressed without words as a deadly silence.

Silence as a Facilitator of Communication

Various authors (Kern, 1978; Warren, 1961) view silence in the analytic situation as resistance and, more specifically, as a defense against transference experiences. However, we posit that silence tends to intensify both transference and countertransference, amplifying the symmetrical and mutually subjective experiences that are attached to that silence. Within the patient's need to give up on words, and to sit in silence with the analyst, can be seen not only the hopelessness and despair of the failure to communicate, but the hope that a real connection might emerge. In our understanding, the *emergence* of a connection needs to be differentiated from the *creation* of a connection.

In the case of Lynn as an example, the "real connection" already existed in the symmetrical mode, although in the asymmetrical mode a rupture in connection was felt. As both Lynn and her analyst consciously were attuned to a verbal (asymmetrical) coding of experience, the real connection needed an opportunity to emerge into the asymmetrical realm where it might be explicated linguistically and brought to conscious awareness. In this case silence constituted this opportunity. The unconscious sharing of subjectivities between Lynn and her analyst was brought to light through the anaclitic translation of symmetrical experience through silence.

In terms of this patient in particular, a "good obsessive" who used words well and defensively, the verbal asymmetrical medium of psychoanalysis served to insulate against deeper symmetrical layers of experience. These deeper layers were expressed through the deadened, lifeless relational quality present in the analysis (the dead mother introject), and in the threatening maternal representation contained in the parallel dreams of analyst and patient. The deadness was translated into the parallel dream imagery via the unfolding of symmetry into an anaclitic/asymmetrical modality, but its more direct symmetrical relation was expressed in the deadened, lifeless, and nonverbal quality of the analytic relationship.

For Lynn, silence was felt to be safe and comforting, at the same time that she worried that her silence would invoke the analyst's rage at her. It seems that the medium of silence itself, although anxiety producing for the analyst, formed a bridge between Lynn's subjective experience and the analyst's subjective experience. Through access to the intense affects that arose in the analyst, the analyst came to know something of where the patient lived unconsciously. Part of Lynn's unconscious communication to her analyst was that she needed the analyst to be quiet in order for the communication to be heard; their verbal communication obscured the more necessary primitive communication. Lynn's silence was an unconscious enactment of what she needed from her analyst. In becoming silent, Lynn unconsciously became the analyst and the analyst, by dreaming a dream for the analysis, unconsciously became the patient. In the moment of the dream, psychically, the analyst and Lynn were one. While they were both frightened, helpless, and alone in the dreams, the analyst knew the mother was threatening. In harboring Lynn's unarticulated experience, she became Lynn as well as herself, for only Lynn could truly know her mother's threat.

The initial connections made by the analyst were also unconscious ones, through the images of the dream. It is the analyst in her dream who reaches out to Lynn, although on another level, it is Lynn, through her silence, who reaches out to her analyst, despite the appearance of disconnection and withdrawal. Until the dreams were shared explicitly, both the murderous rage that endangered both analyst and analysand in their parallel dreams, and the shared subjectivity embedded in their detachment, were dissociated aspects of the analytic dyad. Yet, concurrently, these were active elements of their unconscious relationship.

Within an object-relations context, the silence can be seen as an enactment of the paranoid-schizoid position. For this patient, the integrations that are part of the process of working through the depressive position were impeded as persecutory fears and corresponding schizoid defenses began to take hold in the analytic alliance. Klein (1955), in pointing to the close link between ego integration and object relations, speaks of loving and being loved as constituting integrative experiences. Correspondingly, warding off hatred and persecution leads to ego splitting and withdrawal from the object world, at the same time that the idealized object is preserved. For Lynn, bad-mother introjects and the need to keep the mother safe and idealized constituted persecutory fears within the analytic relationship. Her withdrawal into silence both preserved the analyst from the "lush-green/ green-poison" mother and simultaneously recreated the dead silences of her inner "bad mother." The enactment of that dead silence in the analytic relationship was the affective medium for identifications between analyst and analysand, operating through experiences of futility, deadness, and hopelessness.

The silence can also be seen as creating the medium for the projective identifications of the dream, stimulating both the patient's and the analyst's persecutory fears. Simultaneously, the silence can be seen as a part of the projection—part of what is projected is who is to be silent. The projective identificatory process, as expressed in the unconscious construction of the parallel dream to a conscious sharing of psychic contents in the analysis, paved the way for depressive issues to emerge and paranoid-schizoid regression to ease. From a framework of subject relations, these identificatory relational modes enabled analyst and patient to experience being one another, that is, each experiencing the other momentarily as *of* the self, rather than holding the other psychically *within* the self. The boundaries between the psyches of self and other fell away and the participants found themselves embedded in like subjectivities. In this case, Lynn and her analyst did "find their selves" anew through feeling embedded in the psychic surround of each other.

The Shared Dream as both Parallelism and Mutuality

What enabled the patient and analyst to dream together in this way? From an understanding of identificatory processes, parallel dreams are a milieu for concordant identifications to develop and to be explicated in the analytic relationship. The dreams and the sharing of the dreams between analyst and analysand mobilized the transformation of a more complementary situation to one of concordant identification. Negative introjects, which previously had been forbidden expression in the treatment because of fear and dread of their destructive potential to the analytic dyad, were able to find their way into the analysis through subjective identificatory relatedness between the patient and the analyst.

We might speak, also, of the parallel dream in terms of a self-other dialectic. In dreaming, the self is immersed in subjective experience. On waking, on cognizing, we then move to objective experience, wherein the experience of the subject is momentarily lost and dreams are often forgotten. In all dream states, boundaries between self and other fade; in mutual dream states, they disappear. When mutual dreams are recalled, they occupy a transitional space between verbal expression associated with objectivity and asymmetry and fully symmetrical subjective experience.

In a sense, the term parallel dreams is a misnomer. To borrow from Wilner (1996b), neither parallel lines nor parallel processes meet. Parallel dreams are only parallel to the extent that they are experienced as individual phenomena. From a wholistic standpoint, they are more mutual than parallel. In referring to the separate dream states of two individuals, the term "parallel dreaming" communicates the asymmetrical focus that moves into the foreground in conscious, waking life. It does not express the dedifferentiation of parallel experiences that accompanies shared dreaming. The term "mutual dream" is more appropriate from a symmetrical perspective. It is only in the asymmetrical light of day, so to speak, that the individual aspects of parallel dreaming become more recognizable than their mutuality.

Wilner's (1991) earlier concept of communion has particular relevance for mutual dream phenomena and is congruent with the concept of multidimensional symmetry. As described in an earlier chapter, communal experience emerges spontaneously and outside of conscious awareness between individuals immersed in a mutual psychological context. Communion involves an experiential recognition of the essential wholeness of things and of one's existence as part of the whole.

Parallel dreamers partake of this kind of communal experience. Parallel dreaming is closer to one dream having been dreamt by two people than two people having individual dreams. The process of parallel dreaming expresses the embeddedness that underlies the interpersonal relationship of the dreamers. The bifurcation of symmetrical relational experience into two nearly identical dreams dreamt by two people represents one level of the unfolding process. At another level, related unconscious experience is divided further into the dream elements themselves. Asymmetrical logic distinguishes and sequences unconscious symmetrical experience, reflecting in asymmetrical terms only portions of the symmetrical engagement of the dreamers. At yet another level, these dream images are translated into language, language being the premier asymmetrical function. The symmetrical interpenetrations between the dreamers now are partially accessible to asymmetrical perception and conscious investigation, but at the cost of their wholeness.

Although object-relations theories address projective and introjective processes that can make some sense of parallel dreaming, they are reliant on asymmetrical principles and as such cannot
incorporate the basic lack of differentiation that this phenomenon
expresses. Since they assume that the patient and analyst communicate from separate psychic positions, they are locked into an
asymmetrtical position. They do not consider the possibility that
psychic experience is shared and unitary and that intellectual
awareness of it requires distinctions between self and other that
are misleading derivatives of a deeper psychical commonality.
Thus, notions such as projection and introjection can only explain
phenomena superimposed upon the division of self and other.
Due to their rootedness in the premise of separate psyches, these
concepts cannot shed light on more unitary dimensions of the related unconscious. An appreciation of subject relations is required
to illuminate this sense of unity.

The primitive communication between Lynn and her analyst
did not so much bridge a gap between them as reflect their shared
psychical context. The mutual dream made consciously accessible
their unconscious relatedness, allowing a deeper empathic connection to be recognized within the analytic space. Through
symbolizing shifts between objective and subjective relational
identificatory modes, the dream imagery provided a transitional
experience between symmetrical and asymmetrical modes of
being. Mutual dreams and parallel dreaming, as do other forms of
unconscious communication, afford the analyst the opportunity
to experience the object (the patient) as the subject (the self).
They capture the quality of the related unconscious wherein the
object is defined by what the subject feels.

4

THE UNCONSCIOUS CATCH IN PSYCHOANALYTIC SUPERVISION

Naomi Rucker and Karen Lombardi

It has been recognized for many years that supervisory experiences often are meaningfully related to the experiences between patient and analyst. The concept of parallel process (Searles, 1955) entered the clinical vernacular as a description and explanation for this phenomenon. Parallel process refers to the reflection of transferential and countertransferential aspects of the patient-analyst relationship within the supervisory setting. What the supervisor and supervisee experience with one another parallels the feelings between analyst and patient. Sometimes these parallels are easily detectable, while in other instances, they are more disguised. The catch phenomenon is related to, but distinctly different from, parallel process.

The supervisory relationship aids not only in the reconstruction of dynamics between patient and analyst but also serves as a catch for experience that has been dissociated by both patient and analyst. The elements of this dissociation are not repeated in the analyst-supervisor dyad, as in parallel process, but are carried into it unconsciously so that they can be managed there. Through the analyst, the supervisor absorbs dissociated experience that the patient cannot tolerate internally and that cannot be contained within the analyst-patient relationship. Hence, the analytic relationship is freed from introjects and affects that it cannot metabolize. The interpersonal manifestations of these affects are inactive in the patient-analyst dyad, and present only in the supervisory relationship.

On an object-relations level, the catch process can be conceptualized as a revival of the patient's early primary relationships and the unconscious evocation of others as proxies for the identifications that arise from those relationships. The unconscious hope of the patient-analyst duo is that certain dissociated representations can be contained and metabolized by the supervisor in a manner that still allows all participants sufficient connection to their deeper selves and to each other that a semblance of wholeness can be attained. This process is a triadic solution to a dyadic anxiety; it balances the threats of self-fragmentation and dyadic rupture with a degree of distance from one's toxic internal identifications.

Viewed from a subject-relations perspective, catch experiences radiate from the shared unconscious field of patient, analyst, and supervisor. Facets of symmetrical being are brought into conscious asymmetrical awareness through words, the premier means of translation from symmetrical to asymmetrical experience. The unconscious catch phenomenon is embedded within a wholistic psychic experience to which parallel process does not refer. Parallel processes or lines do not meet in either psychological or physical space (Wilner, 1996b). To explain catch phenomena, we need to look toward wholistic models of experience.

The following series of clinical examples illustrate the unconscious catch in different ways, but before these are detailed it is

important to note the prevalence of patients' unconscious awareness of the presence of a supervisor in their analyst's life. It is almost commonplace for patients to speak metaphorically of a
supervisor of whom they have no conscious knowledge. One patient referred to images of "all-knowing Gods who can't be seen
or heard, but who will eventually hear my silent prayers," while
another analysand had a dream of seeing a shadow on the wall of
his analyst's office that he could not touch. Although these associations bear relevance to each patient's individual dynamics, they
can also be understood as an unconscious acknowledgment of a
supervisory presence. The patients in the first and last examples
offer a clinical illustration of this phenomenon. The first patient is
the young dreamer of the "shadow" dream.

David

David, an artist, was experiencing a constructive analysis and
an affectionate bond with his analyst. In contrast, the analyst was
undergoing a disruption in an otherwise positive relationship
with his supervisor. The analyst was feeling inexplicably dis-
paraged and self-conscious, and was finding it difficult to share
his work candidly. The patient, however, was associating readily
and was seemingly quite self-expressive. The problem with the
supervisor was discussed during supervision as a possible parallel
process and also as an interpersonal difficulty peculiar to the
supervisory dyad. The verbal material brought to analysis by the
patient did not seem to correspond to the supervisory experience,
nor did exploration of the analyst-supervisor exchanges shed
much light on the problem. The analyst's attempts to explore the
situation in his own analysis also were frustrating. After many
weeks, the analyst began to feel resigned to his anxiety in this situation and to attribute it to issues unresolved within himself, in
combination with a mismatch in his choice of supervisor. The supervisor began to feel skeptical of the analyst's continued denials
that anything seemed amiss in the analysis. The supervisor became aware of his growing criticalness and impatience with the
analyst.

At this juncture, the patient received an unexpected visit from
his father. During this visit, the father verbally humiliated him

and harshly criticized one of David's sculptures. The patient feelingly reported his hurt and surprise at his father's behavior. David stated that he had not experienced his father as berating as this before, but eventually began to realize that he had never before shared his sculpture with his father. Previously, the father had seen only David's paintings or drawings, to which he had responded in an indifferent manner. During adolescence, David began to keep his work more private and also began to develop the interest in sculpture that came to be his primary artistic endeavor in adulthood. Much later in analysis, it came to light that David's father was often the spokesman in the family—the "heavy"—for other's suppressed and unspoken judgments.

Upon hearing this clinical material, the supervisor recognized the similarity between the patient's self-protective reaction to his unconscious sense of his father's ability to hurt him, evident in the privacy with which he shrouded his adolescent artistic pursuits, and the analyst's anxiety about being forthright with the supervisor. Neither David's self-protective needs, nor his critical internal introjects, were evident transferentially. David did not seem to fear reproof from the analyst, nor was his need for privacy from his father expressed toward the analyst.

Instead of creating an analytic alliance that reflected his critical internal representations, David developed a relationship with his analyst that felt warm and comfortable. The critical internal objects that were present unconsciously for David had been displaced onto the supervisory context via the analyst. The analyst psychically held both the patient's disapproving imagoes and his isolative protectiveness. The representations of disapproval were transmitted unconsciously to the supervisor for the supervisor to embody, while the analyst embodied the patient's vulnerability. The persecutory introjects, thus, bypassed the analysis. David's toxic representations of his father were not reflected from the analysis to the supervision, as would be the case in parallel process, but were segregated from the analyst-patient relationship to rest within the supervisor-supervisee dyad. The supervisor subjectively identified with and personified the patient's critical-father-introject, discovering in himself the disapproval and fear of injury that David discovered in his father, while the analyst subjectively identified with and personified the vulnerable-David.

Invoking the supervisor as a repository for his dissociated experience was an unconscious compromise for David. He risked self-alienation for safety and distance from that which he most feared. Through his unconscious relationship to the supervisor, David was able to shield himself and share himself simultaneously. He could protect the analytic bond from contamination by hostility and narcissistic injury, while reaching the shadow of himself he needed to feel more complete. Through his "shadow" dream, David alluded to someone else in his history and in his current life with whom he could not connect, but from whom he could not escape. This someone was both his father and his analyst's supervisor.

Ginny

A female analyst had been working with a middle-aged woman in psychoanalysis for a few months, during which time the analyst had been in supervision with a male supervisor. The analysand, Ginny, was described by her analyst as a matronly woman with an unusually prim, but self-effacing, attitude toward the world. Frequently, she was overly apologetic to others and preoccupied with their well-being at the expense of her own. She was chronically alert to others' opinions of her and adhered strongly, and even self-righteously, to social convention and propriety. The analyst felt rather blandly towards Ginny. She found Ginny's conformity rather pedantic and boring at times, and found herself reacting with much less emotion than was usual for her in her work. Her contact with her supervisor was pleasant and cordial, but rather bland and formal. The supervisor felt slightly detached from both her supervisee and from Ginny.

Given this emotional tone, the supervisor found himself perplexed by a growing irritation he began to feel towards his supervisee. When the analyst once arrived quite late for their supervision session without offering an excuse or apology, he experienced her as entitled, condescending, and inconsiderate, and reacted inwardly with anger and contempt. His reaction felt, even to him, more intense than her behavior warranted, and he did not disclose his feelings. The supervisor's perception of the analyst, however, continued to puzzle him for a few weeks, despite their mutual sense that the clinical work with Ginny was progressing satisfactorily, albeit slowly. His perception of the analyst and his emotional reaction to her lateness seemed inconsistent with the cool, but respectful, tenor that had otherwise characterized their relationship.

During this period, the analyst reported that Ginny had noted that the analyst seemed to be "developing some feelings for her." This phrase startled the supervisor, although he could not immediately identify what struck him about it. Overtly, it seemed to be an odd description of the rather inert connection that had existed between patient and analyst, but it seemed to herald a welcome optimistic shift in the quality of their relatedness. Suddenly, it occurred to the supervisor that the words "developing some feelings for her" could be heard in two ways, the most obvious being a growing sense of engagement that perhaps Ginny was experiencing between her analyst and herself. The second meaning of those words conveyed a sense that the analyst was incubating some of Ginny's feelings, literally developing them for her. The deep structure of Ginny's statement carried the unconscious meaning of the blandness between Ginny and her analyst, of the recent shifts in the supervisor's reaction to the analyst, and of some of the meaning of the analyst's lateness. Unconscious aspects of the analytic relationship generated a conscious sense of dormancy or stagnancy related to this incubation, while activity and movement was displaced onto the relationship between analyst and supervisor.

Ginny's self-effacing, apologetic stance towards the world disguised her disavowed sense of narcissism and entitlement, her rage and envy of others who could act upon their needs selfishly, and her unconscious wish to demand the kind of treatment she felt she deserved from those around her without taking any personal responsibility. These feelings were neither accessible in Ginny's conscious experience of herself, nor present in the analytic relationship proper. Rather, they were carried unconsciously by the analyst into her supervisory dyad. The analyst, in relation to her supervisor, personified Ginny's dissociated feelings by presenting herself through her lateness as a tempered version of the unconscious-entitled-Ginny. The analyst behaved in a mildly inconsiderate and entitled way that breached propriety, something that Ginny, consciously, would be loathe to do. This behavior evoked angry disdain in the supervisor, the type of reaction that Ginny fiercely avoided. Thus, patient, analyst and supervisor unconsciously cocreated, personified, and enacted a scenario that represented Ginny's unconscious relational position, bringing to the foreground her dissociated narcissitic identifications.

Doug

Doug was a pudgy young man with a likeable, childlike manner that his therapist found endearing. He had been called by his baby name, "Dougie," most of his life by his family, and experienced this as an expression of his parents' and siblings' affectionate protectiveness toward him. Notably, this information was one of the few details that the therapist had learned about Doug's early life. Doug always focused more on the feelings and events in his current life, giving only passing attention to childhood matters. Interestingly, this patient occasionally would comment to his therapist that he felt as if there were someone else in the office with them, "a ghost."

Doug's therapist was in supervision with a senior analyst whose first name was also Douglas, and she referred to him as Douglas. The supervisor's experience of Doug was quite different from the analyst's. He experienced Doug through the therapist as irritatingly passive, asexual, and infantile, reminiscent of the kind of boys that would be cruelly teased at school. The therapist often felt in the position of defending Doug from her supervisor's harsh perceptions of him. She felt mainly sympathy and compassion for her patient and could not understand her supervisor's reactions.

One day, upon leaving her supervisory session, the therapist bid goodby to her supervisor by inadvertently calling him "Dougielas," rather than her customary "Douglas." She was immediately embarrassed and made uneasy by her mistake, but she realized that it must have much meaning. The therapist recognized the humiliation and hostility she conveyed in calling her supervisor by an infantile name and came to her next supervision session with apology in hand. The supervisor pointed out to her that not only might it have been aggressive towards him, but that her embarrassment and distress about it might bear some connection to her work with Doug.

The therapist responded that she hated how "mortified and small" her error made her feel. As she stated this, the therapist became aware that not only did she hate those feelings in herself, but that she hated them in Doug. Not only did she feel empathy and compassion for him, but she was capable of hating him for his spinelessness, passivity, and immaturity. As supervisor and supervisee discussed this further, it became clear that the supervisor's feelings about Doug had served to express the disgust and intolerance towards Doug that neither the therapist, nor Doug, could openly feel or allow into their mutually created understanding and closeness.

On an unconscious subjective level, Dr. Douglas/Dougielas was Dr. Dougie*less*. As the member in the triad with the least overt connection to Doug, he was "less Doug." He also held the subjective experience of disavowed phantasies and wishes to destroy the "Dougie" in Doug, wishes for Doug to become "less Dougie" (as in minus the Dougie part of Doug). These disowned aggressive feelings were present unconsciously in Doug, his therapist and, speculatively, in Doug's parents. The therapist had identified with the embarrassed, humiliated Dougie who protected himself and his family with a conscious conviction that they were only affectionate and protective toward him. The supervisor had come to embody the phantom ("ghost") dissociated feelings of hatred and loathing that threatened to destroy Doug and that also, because of their dissociation, impeded his psychic growth and integration.

UNCONSCIOUS RELATEDNESS IN MULTIDIMENSIONAL CONTEXTS

The parallel-process paradigm artfully explains the displacement of feelings and processes from the analytic domain to the supervisory arena. It requires, however, some representation of the feelings, phantasies, or impulses within the analysis. It cannot account for material dissociated from the analysis proper. It cannot explain reasons for, or processes through which, the supervisor catches the dissociated experience. For this understanding, we must look to the realm of the related unconscious.

In many instances of the unconscious catch, as in the examples of David and Doug, the patient has no conscious awareness or knowledge of the analyst's supervision. To assimilate the clinical data that we are describing, one must accept that psychic experience can be mutually experienced without awareness and that patients unconsciously can and do harbor knowledge of the analysts' life and personality to which they have no direct access. Clinical anecdotes to this effect are present in the literature under a broad spectrum of psychic correspondences in psychoanalysis (Eisenbud, 1970; Lombardi and Rucker, 1991; Wilner, 1991).

Wilner's idea of communion is most in concert with the hypothesis of multidimensionality of experience, an idea which has been posed by theorists within and outside of the purvue of psychoanalysis (Civin and Lombardi, 1990; Shlain, 1991). According to this hypothesis, objective reality is subordinate to a universal and infinite layering of dimensions of experience. As multiple dimensions shift in and out of the foreground of understanding, attributions that define everyday reality lose prominence, altering experience and perception. Shlain depicts these processes as the impetus for an emerging cultural and scientific Zeitgeist wherein context defines reality. He echoes the sentiment that mind and universe complement one another; neither can exist alone.

Sensitivity to many experiential dimensions is possible only when we detach ourselves from the concrete principles that structure our perceptions of the world. The heightened affect states occurring in psychoanalysis lend themselves to the experience of a multidimensional connectedness beyond that explicable by ordinary unconscious dynamics. Matte-Blanco's (1975) conception of the unrepressed unconscious and its multiple experiential layers and Civin and Lombardi's (1990) theory of infinite dimensionality detail psychic mechanisms for the transformation of unconscious process into conscious awareness. Models of multidimensionality such as these offer the most complete scaffolding for the theoretical construction of unconscious relational phenomena such as the supervisory catch.

Catch experiences are most explicable if we construe patients, analysts, and supervisors as part of a multidimensional psychological field that is created through a myriad of identificatons and disidentifications. Within a framework of object relations, uncon-scious communication among the supervisory participants can be construed to occur via complementary identifications. The pa-tient, in his inability to tolerate certain internal representations, projects them onto the analyst in order to disidentify from them. Through his inability to experience his own concordant identifi-cations, the analyst unconsciously carries these projections into the relationship with the supervisor. In doing so, the analyst disidentifies with the content of the patient's projections, but identifies concordantly with the process of projection in which the patient engages. The material that is caught within the super-vision has been disowned by both patient and analyst and is re-ceived by the supervisor through her concordant identification. Assuming that the supervisor's level of integration allows for the experience and identification with these disowned feelings, they can now be synthesized, first within the shared supervisory space and then by the analyst and patient together and individually. The covert concordance upon which this process depends represents the subjective relational link between patient, analyst, and super-visor that defines related unconscious dimensions.

As projective identificatory processes and object relations pre-sume psychic separateness, they cannot account for the immersion in the projections of another that leaves one without a sense of differentiation from these projections. This immersion requires a subject-relational understanding. Within the constructs of sym-metry, communion, and subject relations, psychic differentiation does not exist. Projective and introjective identifications, which imply the crossing of a separation between individuals, recede as explanatory constructs in favor of the subject-relational concepts of objective and subjective identificatory modes of relating. These lat-ter identifications do not bridge a gap between persons as much as represent the relational mode through which a mutual context is experienced. This understanding gives credence to the idea that gaps cannot be experienced in deeper psychic life. Rather, spaces or gaps are artifacts of differentiation, characteristic of asymmetrical thought that are superimposed upon a substrate of homogeneity and unity. In deeper, more inclusive dimensions, individuals iden-tify subjectively and/or objectively with psychical experience. Catch

experiences, through their requisite concordant identifications, illuminate the subject-relatedness of patient, analyst, and supervisor,
and elucidate the communal context in which their individual subjectivities are one.

TRANSFORMATIVE FUNCTIONS OF SUPERVISION

Within the supervisory triad, the analyst experiences the patient deeply enough to hold and transmit unconscious states, while
the supervisor's unconscious role demands a more indirect engagement. As others in a baby's environment may shield the mother-
infant dyad from demands and intrusions from the external world,
so may the supervisor unconsciously protect the analyst and his
charges from dissociated experience that they are yet unprepared
to integrate. On a conscious, asymmetrical level, supervisors are
overseers of the analytic process as the word supervision (supervision) implies. Unconsciously, however, they afford the opportunity for the integration of encapsulated affect, by providing a net
for psychic material that cannot be assimilated within the analytic
relationship. They hold for safekeeping the unconscious affects
that neither analyst, patient, nor their dyad can embrace. Supervisors share a mutual psychic space with both the analysts and patients that they supervise. When the supervisor unconsciously
catches a fragment of the patient's psychic life, the supervisor is
closer unconsciously to the patient than the patient is to himself.

The analysts in the examples presented did not only carry into
supervision dissociated psychic elements from their patients, but
brought symmetrical relations to the forefront of the predominantly asymmetrical realm of analytic supervision. The supervision process in each of these cases served an unfolding function,
extracting and reflecting the symmetrical properties of the mutual
subjective relatedness of analyst, patient, and supervisor. This unfolding function represented a transformative process that culti-
vates the integration of disparate modes of being within each
individual and the integration of dissociated experiences among
the supervisory parties. The unfolding process thus carries both
individual and relational importance.

Language, the preeminent mode of anaclitic translation and the dominant feature of both analysis and supervision, brought to light Ginny's deeply unconscious sense of narcissistic entitlement, David's persecutory introjects, and Doug's urges to destroy aspects of himself. Language has individual meaning and individual expression in the form of thought, but interpersonal meaning and communicative expression in the form of words. It is perhaps preeminent in anaclitic translation not only because it defines the human species on a psychophysiological level, but also because it is a manifestation of the dialectical nature of the relational pulls that are endemic to the human condition. Language allows us to be separate at the same time that we are connected to others. Language is a simultaneous expression of our apartness and our togetherness, it can create both distance and closeness, and it can both obscure and clarify communication.

The unconscious exchange of psychical experience that occurs in the catch phenomenon is a reminder to us that the verbal qualities of analytic work and supervision convey only a piece of the multiple layers and dimensions that are embedded within clinical relationships. At times, words can become a distraction from the affects that reside within the related unconscious. Yet, it is also through verbal interchange in supervision and analysis that we often can decipher unconscious relational meaning and find our way to deeper understanding. The interpenetration of subjectivities in all three of the case illustrations presented was not telepathic, mystical, or incomprehensible, but simply an expression of our deepest unconscious unity, indivisibility, and subject-relatedness. The delineation of patient, analyst, and supervisor, and of their individually experienced subjectivities, is an expression of the disunity and divisibility that is inevitable in the human condition and that is necessary to both private thought and interpersonal relatedness.

5

THE MUTUAL CREATION OF TEMPORAL EXPERIENCE

Karen Lombardi

> Time present and time past
> Are both perhaps present in time future
> And time future contained in time past
>
> —T.S. Eliot, *The Four Quartets*

The concept of time has occupied a central position in the history of psychoanalytic thought. Developmental theory, from classical and ego psychological perspectives, views time as discontinuous, with the individual moving from one stage of development to the next in a linear or hierarchical fashion. In the movement in time from one stage of development to another, the task of the individual is to master those conflicts posed by the dominance of one erotogenic zone or another, so as to be free to move unencumbered to the next stage of development. In this view, time is seen as discontinuous and, ideally, unidirectionally forward moving; movements back in linear time are seen as regressive and disruptive to the progression of development. Increasing data from infant observational research, and the reformulations of Stern (1985) and others, challenge views of human development that are framed in terms of stage theory, and support the idea that relational issues exist continuously over time.

Similarly, in clinical theory, classical and ego psychological perspectives are dominated by the metaphor of the archeological dig, where the function of the analyst is to help uncover repressed memories from the past, and to release the patient from those unconscious conflicts that fixated him in the past and impeded his free movement in the present. In this view, transference, as the distortion of present by past, is primarily a tool of the dig.

Relational, and particularly interpersonal, clinical theories have focused not so much on unearthing memories and conflicts from the past that impede the present but on the interactions in the transference-countertransference matrix in the here and now. This matrix, containing the immediate lived experience of relational patterns that are derived from the past and contained in the present, is the forum for the investigation of selective repetitions of interactions in which the patient's participation typically has been dissociated.

In subject-relational theory, analyst and analysand are seen as subjects in nonlinear time, not only fusing past and present in the articulation of the analytic relationship, but also creating a new past and a new present. The goal of such an analysis is to move from the self as object to the self as subject, and to the other (the analyst, in this case) as subjectively experienced. This interplay between self and other as objects and self and other as subjectively perceived, mutually create temporal experience. To borrow from Ogden (1994), temporal space exists in both diachronic (temporally sequential) and synchronic modes, with a dialectical interplay between interpenetration of self and other (subjective experience) and the schizoid and autistic-contiguous modes of experience (the self as object). To refer to Matte-Blanco (1975), diachronic time would exist in the realm of asymmetry, whereas synchronic time would be a more anaclitic mode, reflecting more symmetrical process.

The concepts of object, subject, and subjective experience as we are attempting to explore them here require some elaboration. The next section begins with a set of questions, from which follow some provisional responses.

THE TEMPORAL, THE SUBJECTIVE, AND REALITY

The French preoccupation with narcissistic cathexis of the ego at one pole and object cathexis at the other represents the struggle to conceptualize subject and object in terms of self experience, both internally and culturally constructed. In this account, subjectivity and objectivity are formed in dyadic experience, with self standing in contrast to other: "the subject-object pair is formed in a single development: the object as that through which need comes to be satisfied; the subject as that which knows desire and feels alive as the seat of desire" (Viderman, 1980, p. 184). Consistent with the concept of object cathexis in drive theory, the objectified other is the aim of the drive; the possessor of the drive (and the possessor of desire) is the one who possesses subjectivity. When, however, it is the aim which is in itself the object, and not the satisfaction of need, does that set the stage for the transformation of object into subject? Can there then be subject-object pairs? How are they constituted, and in what relation does desire stand in such situations? With regard to internal states, when is the self an object, and treated as an object, that is, objectified, and when is the self subjectively perceived and subjectively experienced? Is the object the subject, treated projectively? And, similarly is the subject the incorporated object? Might subjectivity be constituted through successive incorporations of the object?

If the concept of the object is schematized so that Reality = Externality = Object, then the experience of the object is that it exists in a reality external to the self, which belongs to the world of things. If the subject is schematized so that Ideality = Internality = Subject, then subjective experience, or the experience of the self as subject, is one of inner reality that is projected from the internal to the external world by the subject.

This schematization is consistent with Kleinian theory, which places the distinction between subject and object as equivalent to the distinction between internal and external reality. In Freudian theory, and particularly in ego psychology, there is external reality only; internal states are considered to be conflicts between id and external reality. This conflictual process gives rise to the ego, a representative, however weak, of external reality. The subject-object relationship, according to Freud, is characterized in terms of id-dominated behavior seeking discharge (the subject) onto the tension-reducing sexual object. The subject is the equivalent to (or at least resides in and is dominated by) the id, which represents the world only in terms of its immediate needs, through discharge and distortion of the external world. "Freud's conception of development requires that the subject and object be bifurcated into alien realms of internal and external being" (Feffer, 1982, p. 147).

In Kleinian and subject-relations theory, by contrast, the subject and object live in a state of continuous interplay wherein, through introjective-projective cycles, one constitutes the other; similarly, reality and ideality, externality and internality, constitute variants on poles of a dialectical interplay wherein one is continually constituting the other. The development of subjectivity requires that the individual be empathically experienced through the other as a subject (Winnicott, 1965). One, then, is able to reclaim those parts of the self that are projected into the other, thereby fostering integrative processes, and moving self experience from objectification (that which is projectively experienced, the "not-I") to subjectification (that which is subjectively experienced, the "I"). Klein's "science of the subjective" (Hinshelwood, 1991), a phenomenological approach to the mind and to human relationships and relatedness, requires that the individual be empathically experienced by the other, in order to claim the self as subject.

The critical elements here, in terms of differences in theory, concern varying views of reality, and of the occupation of the subject within the constituted reality. In the positivist view of reality, truth is sought in the objective world. In this view the objectification of experience is valorized; the subjective is considered to be distorted by desire, and is therefore somehow not true, or at least alienated from the objective. The alternative is a constructivist or relativistic view of reality, where subjective experience both creates and partakes of external reality, so that, as in Kleinian psychology, there is not reality and id distortion, but internal or psychic reality and external reality. When the links between the internal and external are strong, there is less need to rely on projection to create an external world that is dissociated from the self. In this latter view, subject and object are not necessarily bifurcated into alien realms of internal or subjective and external or objective reality; the alienation of subject and object are seen in terms of pathology, in terms of weak links or attacks on linking functions (Bion, 1959), and not in terms of necessary, or even idealized and sought after, gaps.

The arguments regarding subject-object and related dialectics posed by classical or relational theory are themselves artifacts of the asymmetrical logic that gives us an intellectual life. However, this logic blinds us to the dimensions of experience in which there are no gaps, valorized or otherwise, and in which there are no discrete elements to be linked through projection or segregated through dissociation. Projection, dissociation, or the like all exist within a realm of experience characterized by disunity and within which the temporal relations that they imply are unformed. Without the concept of time, notions of projection, and dissociation, subject-object shifts cannot be conceptualized.

Within the paradigm posed by Matte-Blanco and from which subject-relations theory emanates, concepts of subject-object, self-other, internal-external, and past-present represent asymmetrical positions extending from symmetrical experience, in which these distinctions have no existence. In fundamental symmetry, being dominates over happening, with experience existing apart from the temporal-spatial connections that happening requires. Self *is* other and other *is* self; internal *is* external and external *is* internal;

subject *is* object and object *is* subject. It is only in the striving for separateness and consciousness that dialectical distinctions are meaningful and the interplay between them takes on temporal characteristics.

Temporality and Its Relation to Space

In the domain of human existence, it is difficult to conceptualize time without space, and without reference to spatial metaphors. Temporal space, which exists on a time/space axis, is most commonly considered to be diachronic, or sequential and linear. Temporal-spatial relations, such as before and after, earlier and later, here and there, fall within the diachronic mode. In this model, which is based on a Newtonian view of the physical world, objects can be located and fixed in space. Diachronic temporality, which often is relied upon to describe movement from past to present in reference to human developmental stages and to psychoanalytic process, describes subject-object relations, and represents the objectification of experience. Diachronicity is linked to distance, both physical and psychic. Notions of the diachronic fit well with theories that describe movement through libidinal phases (Freudian), that describe development of the self from psychic merger or embeddedness to individuation and autonomy (Mahlerian), or that depict development and/or therapeutic change in terms of a necessary sequence of relational experiences (Kohutian). The developmental arrest or deficit model is one of holes in experience creating holes in the self that need to be filled or plugged up in order for development to proceed. Developmental/therapeutic progress within this framework is based on the ability and opportunity to go back in time psychically.

Synchronic temporality, on the other hand, describes a time/space axis that functions dialectically (Ogden), or, perhaps even more aptly, as a spiral. This model, derived from modern physics, reflects the influence of relativity theory and specifically of the Heisenberg principle, which states that the location of an object in space is relative to the perspective of the viewer. In this way, temporal experience cannot be fixed absolutely, but depends on the relative movement of all elements that pertain to the object, as well as to the movement of the object. Synchronicity, a coincidence in point of time, refers to the simultaneity of experience that dominates in more symmetrical dimensions. The distance that characterizes diachronic temporal modes is greatly diminished in synchronic modes; synchronicity represents intimacy, attunement, and movement toward shared subjectivity. Although synchronicity more closely describes subject-subject relations than does diachronicity, it does retain the implication of two discrete events occuring together.

In both paradigms of the diachronic and the synchronic, asymmetry is implicated in the use of space and distance to describe time. The forward progression of diachronic time and the merging of events in synchronic time both equate time with movement across space. However, synchronicity signifies the absence or closing of distance, whereas diachronicity signifies the separation between events. Thus, self-self relations are experienced more in the synchronic mode, in simultaneity and without reference to the distantiated perspective of linear time. Self-object relations, in constrast, are experienced in the diachronic mode, emphasizing distance, objectification, and the otherness which that implies. While the concept of synchronicity can provide an approximate explanation for temporal experience in the subject-relational realm, it is fundamentally limited by its inherent asymmetries.

The dialectic between diachronic and synchronic experience is valuable in understanding the correspondence between objectivity and subjectivity. Ogden (1992a, 1992b, 1994) credited both Freud and Klein with the dialectically constituted/decentered subject. In his view, the subject (and the experience of subjectivity) is the outcome of a process whereby the subject is simultaneously constituted and decentered from itself by means of the dialectical interplay of consciousness and unconsciousness. This constitution of the subject is a particularly psychoanalytic one, wherein consciousness and unconsciousness are seen as mutually dependent, rather than independent of one another, coexisting in a relationship of relative, not absolute, difference. One does not live two lives, one conscious and the other unconscious, but a single life constituted by interplay of conscious and unconscious modes of experience.

Ogden's emphasis on the topographical model allows him to state that the subject, for Freud, is to be sought in the relations between the unconscious and the conscious. However, his relative disregard for the structural model, and for the precept, "Where id was, ego shall be," moves him away from the linear thinking that characterizes many Freudian conceptualizations, particularly those of the ego psychological model that have so influenced American psychoanalysis. While Ogden may state fairly that in Freudian psychology, neither consciousness nor unconsciousness holds a privileged position with regard to the formulation of the subject, placing Freud more in line with ideologies characterized by the relativistic and dialectical, he ignored the preponderance of Freudian thought that is characterized by unilinear movement through space and time. The timelessness of the unconscious is not simply a quality of the unconscious that holds equal status with the linear, positivist, time-space continuum of the conscious. This timelessness is also regarded as a function of the distortion resulting from id pressures. It is desire that creates timelessness, and distorts objective reality through that desire.

Ogden argues for a psychological theory that incorporates both diachronic and synchronic perspectives, and claims that Kleinian and Freudian theories each contain both perspectives. We argue that clinical work exists more within a synchronic than a diachronic frame, although tendencies to value the diachronic over the syn- chronic exist within several major psychoanalytic movements. The ego psychological and Mahlerian schools, and the deficit model, as represented by self-psychology and the early work of the intersub- jectivists, are tied to linear conceptions of the development of the self through time and thus retain a positivist perspective of reality.

The Realm of Achronicity, Symmetry, and Subject Relations

In positing a dialectic between synchronic and diachronic spa- tial-temporal perspectives, Ogden attempts to retain the idea of primary or objective reality. This reality is described or sought after in the domain of the conscious mind, at the same time that he emphasizes the movement from objectivity to subjectivity and back again. In our view, the current discourse on subjectivity continues to suffer from the assumption—often unacknowledged— that there is a static real other or external world to which the individual relates, as if it were possible to freeze psychical process in time and ignore or filter out the perpetual interchange between internal and external, self and other. Many who regard themselves as intersubjectivists, while developing relativistic models of the construction of the self, nevertheless have retained positivist assumptions of the external world, and thus have remained tied to the assumption of an objective externality that can be fixed in time.

The real movement in the relation between subject and object, which Ogden explicates from a Kleinian perspective, is in the dialectics of introjection and projection. Here, the external becomes internal, and the internal is externalized, and both subject and object are continually constituted. In this dialectic, it is the meeting and the matching of internal and external experience that is the fundament of subjectivity. In his zeal to incorporate classical principles into his thinking, Ogden glosses over the inclination to esteem the diachronic over the synchronic. Even when neither is privileged, the diachronic and the synchronic remain different versions of static modes of temporality. Ogden extracts movement from the dialectics between these modes, but this does not quite capture the complexity of subjective experience.

This complexity is better captured by achronicity or timelessness, a feature of symmetrical dimensions, than by either diachronicity or synchronicity, both of which imply some degree of asymmetry. The achronic dimension is the fundament from which both synchronic and diachronic experiences are created and articulated. While distance and the passage of time are implicit in object-relating in either a diachronic or synchronic frame, relatedness in an achronic dimension is characterized by the absence of time or distance and the simultaneous presence of all temporal possibilities. Achronicity depicts the timelessness of experience, the experience of timelessness, and the eternality of the momentary. It exists within the symmetrical dimension encompassing subject relations.

Regression Out of Time

When temporal experience is conceptualized in nonlinear rather than linear terms, the fundamental psychoanalytic concept of regression needs to be reformulated. Freud (1916–17) used the concept of regression to refer specifically to a shift backwards from later psychosexual stages to fixation points in earlier stages of instinctual life. Regression was viewed as movement backwards in psychical time, from present to past, as well as a backwards movement in development, from adult to child, or more specifically, from the genital stage of libidinal development to the phallic, anal, or oral stage. As a backwards movement of the psyche, regression was seen as an undoing of the gains brought about by the forward movement of maturation and development. Freud's stress on overcoming the press of the pleasure principle in favor of increased adaptation to an externally given objective reality led him to view regression as a factor in pathogenesis. In his clinical theory, Freud (1912) viewed regression as a resistance to psychoanalysis, aimed at gratification of instinctual needs, and distinctly opposed to the patient's willingness and ability to work through the transference neurosis. At the same time, Freud exhorted the clinician to welcome regression, as it pointed the way to understanding the patient's conflicts, rooted as they were in the past and enacted in the present with the analyst rather than spoken or understood.

Kleinian theory, in speaking to the continuity of human development through the concept of layered experience, provides an alternative developmental model within which regression may be viewed differently. Central to Klein's view of human development is the assumption that tendencies toward ego integration exist from birth, with sufficient ego to experience anxiety, utilize early defenses and form object relations. The ways in which the object is experienced depends both on external factors and on the sort of internal anxiety that predominates in the individual and come to be projected into the object. The anxieties common to the paranoid-schizoid and depressive positions, respectively, color one's experience in relation to the object. Although Klein's positions represent a developmentally occurring progression from one to the other, they are not stages but positions in relation to the object that shift in emphasis over time. As experiences of object-relatedness, and as felt anxieties in relation to the object, these positions may become modified but are never completely resolved, remaining as potential felt experience that may be evoked through changes in external or internal circumstance. In such layering of experience, there is movement back and forth across varying modes and levels of organization.

According to this view, regression is no longer a simple backward movement in time and in developmental stage, but rather a shift from more differentiated to more dedifferentiated modes of experience. This conceptual orientation is seen even more powerfully in Matte-Blanco's work and in subject-relational assumptions, wherein shifts in differentiation mark the translation between symmetrical and asymmetrical modes and have no essential basis in either temporal progression or level of developmental maturity. Concepts such as process or progression signify the anaclitic translation of achronic experience into diachronic or synchronic temporality. Object-relational experiences, usually described along a developmental continuum that itself is an asymmetrical manifestation, can be created and experienced at any moment in the subjective relational realm. From the layered experiential perspective of subject relations, patient and analyst develop the capacity to experience both themselves and each other in the subjective mode, mutually creating past, present, and future through the eternality of the momentary.

The Scrabble Player[1]

A young man in his first year of community college was mandated into treatment after participating in a group assault of a peer. He was unreflective, did not speak of his own life or experience, and presented no history of continuity of himself in therapy. His intense disavowal of a relationship between himself and the therapist left the therapist feeling that she was alone in her shared relational history with him. The therapist and he came upon playing Scrabble as a form of communication. Though playing the game

---

[1] This example was provided by Frances Roper.

was his idea, it was in some ways the therapist's game, a game of words in which she was the expert. They had been playing Scrabble for several months, coming to experience each other and building a relationship with each other through the vehicle of building words and meaning from scattered fragments.

During one session, the young man played especially well and won the game. He found his victory especially exciting and satisfying since, according to him, it was his first win over her. The therapist told him that she was sure that this was not true; he replied that there was no way of knowing; she said "But I've kept the scores." He was surprised that she had done this, and was curious about what this bit of recorded history would reveal. The therapist went to get the scores and they looked them over together. One or two previous victories of his had been recorded. Both therapist and patient experienced this session as being particularly soothing. The therapist described the session as marking a diminishment in the patient's persecutory anxiety, particularly in the sense that she was a persecutory object and a vanquisher.

In this anecdote, the past is created through experience in the present. The subjective experience of the young man as victor reflected his capacity to share in the identity of the victorious, to recognize in himself something of the identity shared between him and the therapist. Through such experience came acknowledgment of a personal sense of his own continuity, both internally as a young man with a history, and in the therapeutic dyad where there was less need to split off from conscious experience the equations between self and other. In reviewing the scores they became both winners and losers together. Through this symmetrization, time past is created in time present, and parts of the self are both created and regained.

6

THE PRENATAL ANLAGE
OF PSYCHIC LIFE

Naomi Rucker

From the theoretical perspective articulated in this book, the development of selfhood is a process of shifts toward and away from asymmetry. The symmetrical substrate from which a self emerges encompasses multiple dimensions that lie between the symmetrical mode of experience and the presence of asymmetrical codes of logic. One of the most basic gradations is the experience

---

Note: An earlier version of this paper was published in the *British Journal of Psychotherapy*, January 1994, under the title "Reflections of Prenatal Experience in Psychoanalytic Dreams, Imagery and Process."

of being a part of and simultaneously apart from an encompassing surround. Here one may experience only a vague, diffuse, and
fragile sense of separateness that still retains the amorphous character of its symmetrical origins and its roots in subject relations.

Physiologically, this dimension of the move between symmetry and asymmetry is captured by analogy to prenatal life. In
utero, the baby exists within another's body and the baby's
growth is intertwined with another's biological state, yet ongoing development creates increasingly definitive and substantial
boundaries. In this gestational period, the physical self is molded
by and infused with qualities of the (m)other. A psychical analogy exists wherein psychological selfhood is more merged with
that of the (m)other than at any other point in the lifespan. Both
physically and psychically, during gestation, undifferentiation has
yet to give way to the degree of differentiation that hallmarks
postnatal life, yet both separateness and merger are present from
the beginning.

The earliest origins of psychological subjectivity have generally been ascribed to the bodily separation of mother and infant at
birth. Yet, recent investigations have melded the subjective
province of psychoanalytic inference with more objective data on
fetal experience and capacities. Credence is being given to the possibility that a person's sense of self may begin to form before birth
(Stern, 1985; Winnicott, 1988), and prenatal experiences are understood to be formative templates for later experience and relatedness (Verny, 1987). Although many traditional psychoanalytic
thinkers, as well as many developmental experimentalists, still dis-
miss the notion of preverbal subjectivity as beyond the scope of
legitimate inquiry, other prominent thinkers have shown interest
in the nature of prenatal life.

Freud's (1909, 1915) understandings of déjà-vu dreams and
the processes of sleep as recreations of intrauterine existence and
birth, Rank's (1914) theories of birth as the prototype for separation anxiety, Winnicott's (1949, 1954) discussions of intrauterine regression, and Laing's (1976) volume on the meaning and
symbolism of prenatal experience are all instances of the undercurrent of interest in psychoanalysis in prenatal modes of relating.
From a purely philosophical focus, Kant (1781/1965) proposed

the presence of an omniscient substrate of knowledge about ourselves and the objective world, which is independent of sensory experience and is in existence from our earliest uterine beginnings.

Until recently, speculations about fetal life were, by necessity, adultopomorphic. Opportunities for direct observation of fetal development and behavior have been made possible by recent technological advances, such as ultrasound techniques. Such technologies have spurred the genesis of pre- and perinatal psychology as a multidisciplinary field that examines aspects of conception, pregnancy, and birth from both theoretical and empirical bases. Through observational study, a fuller concept of the unborn infant as a conscious, active organizer of the perceptual experiences he or she encounters is emerging (Chamberlain, 1987). Analytic investigators, such as Piontelli (1989, 1992) are tracing and documenting the influences of prenatal psychological life on later emotional development.

In a previous paper, Rucker (1994) presented clinical and theoretical material to support her contention that the residues of intrauterine existence inevitably color postuterine experience, and that echoes of these prenatal motifs can reverberate within the analytic dyad in adulthood. In this chapter, some of this same clinical material will be presented and those ideas will be extended to include the idea that prenatal life is a prototype of the relational unconscious, of subject-object and subject-subject relations, and of the unfolding of symmetrical being into modes of asymmetry. Before the onset of the birth process, psychological relationships that are imbued with affect and carry meaning already exist for the baby. Although the infant's psychical life is peppered with asymmetrical functions, the symmetrical mode of being is ever-present in the baby's experience. Unconscious experiential configurations of symmetry and asymmetry form kernels from which the infant's early self, early relatedness, and later representations are constructed.

FOUNDATIONS FOR THE PREMISE OF PRENATAL SUBJECTIVITY

Freud's (1926) claim that "during intrauterine life, the mother was not an object for the fetus and at that time there were no objects at all" (p. 138) has been challenged by research on pre-natal development discerning perceptual capacities of the fetus and suggesting that bonding between mother and unborn infant is more significantly present than had been thought. As early as 1950, Montague presented data showing that central nervous system (CNS) stimulation from the mother's body led to changes in the endocrine system in the fetus and changes in fetal learning and conditioning. Ploye (1973) and Rottman (1974), cited by W. Ernst Freud (1987), give evidence for the physiological and psychological channels through which a mother's feelings may impact her unborn child.

Chamberlain's (1987) discussion of the research on con-sciousness at birth indicates that some perceptual capacities of the embryo or fetus are present as early as the seventh week of gesta-tion when CNS reflexes can be shown. Facial movements of the fetus indicating approach-avoidance reactions are present at nine to twelve weeks gestation, hearing can be demonstrated by the third trimester of pregnancy, premature infants react to light, and crying has been photographed at twenty-three weeks gestation. Piontelli's (1989, 1992) observational studies of unborn infants and their development through early childhood present the fetus as aware of and involved with the intrauterine surround in ways that become characteristic of subsequent interpersonal relation-ships. Twins in utero display individual tempermental characteris-tics as well as behavioral and interactional patterns that identify them as a pair. These early markers of temperament and twin re-latedness carry over after birth.

Such data suggest that by the latter half of gestation, if not be-fore, the fetus is capable of registering and reacting to experiences within the womb. The notion that fetal life can be recalled experi-entially is supported by the accumulation of data demonstrating capacities for cells to learn, that memory may be stored through-out the cells of the body, not only in the brain, and that memory is retrievable via chemical, electrical, and psychogenic stimulation (Bucheimer, 1987). Such research, although conducted from a vastly different perspective than ours, traces the unfolding of ex-perience from symmetrical to asymmetrical dimensions. The fetus gradually becomes discriminating and differentiated both within his own being and from his maternal environment. In our thinking, fetal states of indivisibility and attachment develop concurrently with distinction of self.

In contrast to experimental investigation of the gestational process, psychoanalytic thinking has been inclined to divorce intrauterine experience from its portrayal of the roots of psychic life. Despite much anecdotal material found in clinical and nonclinical arenas regarding antenatal phenomena—birth memories, vestigial feelings, impressions, sensations stemming from fetal life, mothers' subliminal awareness of pregnancy at the point of conception, people's recollections of events experienced by their mothers only during the pregnancy with them—only infrequently has psychoanalysis taken such material seriously. It is likely that the symmetrical pull of such material is difficult for more asymmetrically geared analysts to digest; perhaps they are more comfortable with material that assumes basic asymmetrical (subject-object) distinctions. Nevertheless, some psychoanalytic theorists have articulated the view that the capacity to encode psychological experience precedes birth and that a dynamic relationship between the embryo and its human surround is experienced from the womb.

Donovan (1989) has created the paradigm of the "paraconscious" to describe a form of cognition dating from embryological life into the first year of infancy. Paraconscious thought is encoded pansensorially, it has no distinct mental representations or content, and its substance is not retrievable at will. In these ways it is similar to Matte-Blanco's symmetrical mode of experience. The paraconscious mode denotes a means of knowing that complements conscious and unconscious thinking, and which arises through a dialectical mutuality between mother and fetus or baby.

The physical and chemical interchanges between mother and fetus and the "primary sensitiveness" of the fetus to its amniotic milieu are theorized by Whyte (1991), Bion (1977), and Klein (1957) to be precursors to and prototypes of later psychological development and object relations. Maizels (1990), Paul (1989, 1990), and Winnicott (1988) address the transition from the intrauterine to postuterine state as central in the development of morality, mood, emotional relatedness, and continuity of being. Balint (1968) regards the cathexis of the uterine environment or surround by the fetus to be more intense than a child's or adult's orientation to the external environment. All of these propositions speak to facets of the symmetrical mode of being.

Balint and Matte-Blanco discuss the meaning of birth from separate, but complementary, perspectives. Balint describes the state of affairs among fetus, amniotic fluid, and placenta as a "harmonious, interpenetrating, mix-up" (p. 66) that is traumatically upset by the process of birth. He likens the fetal-uterine bond to one's later relationship to air—one rarely notices air when it is plentiful, but its removal immediately invokes desperation and threat of death. In Balint's opinion, narcissism is *secondary* to an antenatal state of boundaryless harmony, rather than primary as classically understood. According to Matte-Blanco, birth is made possible by the expression of aggression, aggression being divisive (asymmetrical) by nature. Balint's sense of harmonious interpenetration can be viewed as a primarily symmetrical experience that is ruptured with the physical differentiation and separation that come with birth. By extrapolating from these conceptualizations, narcissism can be viewed as the reaction of a neonatal self to a sudden assault on the sense of symmetrical immersion with the uterine surround that is initiated by the process of birth.

PHENOMENOLOGICAL CONTRIBUTIONS

The symmetrical qualities of fetal life also have been depicted by theorists attuned to phenomenology. Laing (1976) portrayed life inside a womb as the first experience of context and the prototype for later experiences of space, time, relatedness, and mood. Some of his notions are related to Matte-Blanco's later mention of the emergence of basic distinctions at birth. The unfolding process from the symmetrical to the asymmetrical mode that is initiated with birth provides a basic orientation to the spatiotemporal sequencing and heterogeneity indicative of conscious asymmetrical thought.

Laing divides the process of intrauterine gestation into three phases, each of which corresponds to a certain type of existential experience that connotes the nature of the physiological process characteristic of that phase. The richness of his imagery captures the metaphoric, experiential, and homogeneous nature of the un-born infant's psychic surround, and also of the nature of asymmetry. In Laing's descriptions, the period from conception to implantation is expressed in images such as domes, spinning spheres, balloons, planets (blastula); tunnels, drifting down rivers, walking down aisles (Fallopian tubes); being washed away, fears of nonexistence. The stage from implantation to birth is conveyed in metaphors of being sucked in, being welcomed, snuggling into, perishing from fatigue or starvation; drowning; themes of quicksand, swamps; feelings of never getting a grip, putting down roots, just hanging on; fears of being a changeling or of never having felt adequately connected. Birth is represented by feelings of suffocation, entrapment, pressure, waves of terror, helplessness in the face of external forces. In like fashion, Chamberlain (1990) considers tubes, trees, flags and flagpoles to symbolize the umbilical cord and placenta, the conduits between mother and fetus.

It is worth noting that Laing's descriptions capture not only the soothing qualities of life in the womb, but also the potential for destruction and terror. He, along with Klein (1959) and Ploye (1973), recognize the possible negative valence of life in utero. Ploye points out that "good" intrauterine memories, symbolized by such images as idyllic watery surroundings and expressions of blissful oneness, have always enjoyed some acceptability in psychoanalytic theory, but "bad" experiences in the womb are rarely mentioned in the literature. Klein (1957) notes that imagining prenatal life to be purely harmonious may originate in the need to idealize experience. She views persecutory anxieties and envy as representative of insecurities in intrauterine life that are mobilized at birth and foreshadow the dual (good and bad) aspects of the baby's postnatal relationship to his or her mother. As all mothers are far from alike, so may be the uterine milieux they provide. The assumption that life in the womb is essentially safe, warm, nurtu-rant, protective (Guntrip, 1968) may be true for only some embryos in some mothers.

Searles' (1960) contention that infants relate in the earliest days of living to their inanimate as well as their human surround and carry impressions of that experience throughout their lives is an assertion that captures the essence of Matte-Blanco's idea of timeless, symmetrical unity. Searles (1979) suggests that there exists, even in healthy persons, a subjective undifferentiation from the "great inanimate realm of the environment." Unconscious relatedness with inanimate objects implies a sense of sameness and identification with those things that later are objectified and perceived as radically and inherently different from the self. The substrate for unconscious relatedness with the inanimate surround may be found in the fetal experience of the uterine environment.

Conception and fetal development can be understood to occur through a process of simultaneous fragmentation (cell division to create differentiation of function) and integration (cell unification to create coordination in function) that expresses the perpetual dialectical movements between symmetry and asymmetry. At the earliest, most basic levels of experience, unification and differentiation are experienced together. However, the symmetrical mode of being is primary until birth and, within this symmetrical engagement, the fetus and the uterine surround together constitute a whole. Birth signifies the division of fetus-uterus into baby and mother, the ascendence of the asymmetrical mode of being, and ushers in compensatory attempts to restore a sense of harmony and wholeness.

Thus, the first relationship in life may not be with the mother as a person, but with the affective and physiological context that her inner body provides. Her interior space, the fetus' first inanimate object, may provide a container for symmetrical experience. Until birth, this container protects the growing fetus from a precipitous transition between the more symmetrical dimensions of gestation to the more asymmetrical modes evident in postnatal consciousness. The mother and her infant, through her uterine space, are connected within an experiential symmetrical mode where differentiation is minimal and context dominates over contents. The original "holding environment" (Winnicott, 1965) may not be the interpersonal components of the mother-infant relationship, but the mother's interior space as a habitat for the developing self.

The following clinical material illustrates both the symmetrical qualities of intrauterine life and the nascent asymmetry that coexist as fetal development process. These cases also illustrate the manner in which prenatal subjectivity can be echoed in the vicissitudes of an analytic relationship in adulthood.

Jill

Jill was a young woman in her twenties when she began psychoanalysis. Her life had been disrupted by the loss of a romantic relationship and the rise of depression and anxiety that came at its heels. About the third year of analysis, Jill began to speak of impressionistic feelings she had about her early infancy. She felt "hypersensitized" to her mother's emotions towards her and reported affects in their relationship that were inexplicable by the events and memories of her childhood. A feeling that she had been "born sad" and a vague sense of not having been wanted were curiously juxtaposed with memories indicating that Jill was a loved and cherished child.

Preferences for small spaces, close physical contact, and tactile stimulation were threads throughout Jill's life. She reported having had very sensitive skin in early childhood that never became symptomatic dermatologically, but which left her vulnerable to goose pimples and unable to tolerate scratchy fabrics such as wool. Early in her analysis, this symptom reemerged, accompanied by tactile sensations of "hot, tingly" skin and associations to something abrasive or prickly. She experienced occasional interpretations that were imperfectly presented as assaults that "stung," that almost physically hurt the periphery of her body. She was acutely sensitive to the undercurrents of meaning conveyed by the analyst's voice intonation, body posture, and consistency of affect.

Jill recalled being an unusually shy and timid girl who never felt quite prepared to handle the tasks she had to face, although overtly she did quite well socially and academically. Needs for understanding that no one could ever meet left Jill in a fog of longings that she usually kept from her full awareness. When these yearnings did materialize, she would feel desperate for something she could never define and which no one's words or actions seemed to fulfill. Once when this happened during her analysis, the analyst had the sensation and image of Jill becoming smaller and somehow intangible, despite the heightened affects she was displaying. Retrospectively, this moment captured the vagueness of the connection she experienced with her mother prior to her birth, a connection that was disguised by her childhood years of relatedness with loving, adequate parents. Occasionally during the analysis, Jill would dream of fetuses. In one dream, in particular, Jill felt a poignant sense of compassion to the point of tears for unborn babies who were being taken out of their environments prematurely, while no one was attending to their pain.

Jill's mother's pregnancy with her was medically unremarkable. However, she "did not know" she was pregnant until her fourth month. Four days prior to the delivery of Jill, the amniotic sac broke. At that time, because no medical interventions were recommended for this turn of events, Jill's mother was told to go home and wait for contractions. No contractions came for four days. Once labor began, it was long and the baby did not engage properly in the pelvis until many hours of labor had passed. Eventually, Jill was born, a small but healthy infant who for the early weeks of her life cried relentlessly and did not take food readily. From the second month of infancy, Jill began to thrive and to develop into a precocious child with no major signs of psychopathology. As an adult, she functions very well in many areas.

Initial analytic explorations revolved around the dynamics within Jill's family, her affective responses to these dynamics, and their recapitulation in her current relationships. While this line of thinking did have moment and led to insight, understanding, and some relief of her distress, it did not seem to touch the core of Jill's experience of herself. It seemed helpful and relevant, but insufficient. Only when the analyst began look at Jill's' subjective descriptions of her early life in a more literal manner and acknowledge that Jill may have carried traumatic residue of experiences before her birth into her later life, were her more deep-seated emotions and sense of insecurity reachable.

Jill began to verbalize feelings reminiscent of deeply symmetrical experience, feelings of "not being fully formed" and of a sense of being within a closed, abrasive, reddish space in which she existed in a state of diffuse, but acute, discomfort. Within this space she felt unable to differentiate perceptual sensations. She felt herself to be "hearing the warmth" and to be aware of a gray-ish form in the atmosphere that seemed to be everywhere and nowhere at the same time. She reported having felt awash with a deep insecurity that she did not exist.

Interestingly, and not coincidentally, this feeling was paralleled by her mother's obliviousness to her own pregnancy. Jill grew within the body of a mother who was unaware of her existence for the first trimester of her pregnancy. Neither Jill nor her mother were sure that Jill existed. This (literally) existential uncertainty was a shared experience born of their symmetrical union that lived within their related unconscious. Perhaps the shared nature of this insecurity, along with the tentativeness of selfhood in early gestation hindered its integration. Nonetheless, the themes of feeling unwanted, unacknowledged, and isolated from human contact that seemed to contradict many of Jill's childhood recollections were no longer so baffling.

Melinda

Melinda was a strikingly intelligent, successful, and person-able woman in her thirties who came for psychotherapy upon the emergence of chest pains and numbness in the upper left side of her body. Medical assessments were inconclusive, ruling out heart failure, but noting marked tautness in her left side. Physical and psychological therapy were recommended, although Melinda had already entered psychotherapy of her own accord. Her physical therapist noted that the left side of her body "had no life in it." Privately, Melinda feared she would not survive.

Initially, Melinda seemed to be a woman with remarkably few flaws. She was optimistic, highly self-assured, acutely intelligent, and an attractive, likable person with a sense of humor. In her words, she had always had a "voracious appetite for knowledge and learning." Her analyst experienced her as surprisingly self-contained and autonomous. In other words, she appeared to be well-entrenched in asymmetrical modes of functioning. Like her physicians, this analyst was hard-pressed to find enough wrong with Melinda to warrant her symptoms. How to best nourish her was unclear. Melinda seemed too separate and too self-sufficient to be fed by another.

In the initial sessions, the analyst had difficulty in finding areas that might warrant investigation or interpretation, and felt both perplexed and intrigued. Over time it became apparent that it was sometimes hard to intuit Melinda's inner experience from her verbal communications. Although Melinda clearly had emotional vitality and responsiveness and inwardly was able to discriminate nuances of experience, her verbal communication seemed somewhat obscure. Melinda's thinking was not disordered, but she was aware of internal subtleties that she could not express quickly or distinctly enough to be clear. She felt filled with thoughts and feelings that defied words and often felt frustrated and trapped by the limits of communication. Melinda came to describe her style of verbal interaction as "talking cryptic" and the analyst had to learn to "listen cryptic" to follow her. This process between analyst and analysand captured the essentially intuitive and nonverbal level of her interpersonal connections that was present despite her mature psychological integration and intellectual sophistication.

Melinda was one of many children in a middle-class nuclear family, the second-born in a set of identical twins. She grew up in a seemingly related, stable family, with solid family interaction and strong support for academic and athletic endeavors. Melinda was continually a superior student and athlete until several years before starting analysis, when she underwent a "botched" surgery, which left her unable to walk for over a year. Four years before entering analysis, Melinda's parents were killed in a fire and she, the youngest of the siblings, took over all the family affairs with a striking maturity and deftness.

Melinda readily acknowledged that the pains and tightness in her body were manifestations of feelings she could not articulate and which left her constricted and burdened. She stated that she often experienced parts of herself as "someone over there" and would gesture to a space in front and to the left of her chest. During one session, Melinda mentioned that her twin sister had been malnourished and anemic at birth and had not been expected to survive, while Melinda had been robust and healthy. The birth of twins was unexpected. Her mother was told that she might have a uterine tumor that would have to be removed after delivery, but no one anticipated a second infant. (A tumor was expected, but two more were not.) Melinda stated that her joke with her sister had always been that she (Melinda) had kicked her sister out of the womb, elaborating with a smile that she must have wanted a few minutes alone. Her sister did survive and had a normally healthy childhood, but the parents of several young children (including twins, one of whom was gravely ill) must have been overwhelmed.

The interpretation was offered that Melinda's autonomous, driven tendencies may have been established very early as a way for her to cope with a lack of attention. The hypothesis was presented that her sturdiness allowed her parents to see her as okay by herself if given basic care, allowing them to attend to the overtly needier twin and the older siblings. Melinda corroborated that she had always been more mature, responsible, and independent than even her older brothers and sisters and that everyone just expected her to cope. She always did so admirably. The analyst added that perhaps Melinda was not permitted to experience her own needs for attention or concern.

Melinda's thoughts about this material over the next few sessions led her to remark that her mother had had a miscarriage prior to the conception of the twins and that she (Melinda) had always felt deep down that she should have been that aborted baby. In the context of this phantasy, it is interesting that she described her surgery as "botched." Melinda also reported a conviction that she should have been a singleton, experiencing herself as a whole that had been divided into parts. Here in this phantasy of being a divided whole lies a pocket of symmetry.

Melinda's subsequent associations to herself as a divided ovum led to the divisions within her psychological self, the separations between her physical symptoms and her psychological well-being, her intuition and her analytic mind, the left and the right sides of her body. She also stated that her emotions, while subjectively felt, were "shriveled up" and not fully alive, like the upper left quadrant of her body, like her malnourished twin sister and like her mother's supposed tumor. One meaning of these associations may be that Melinda's prenatal embeddedness in symmetry gave way too quickly and too abruptly to asymmetrical experience. Perhaps her associations to self-division are an unconscious reference to the disruption of a symmetrical mode of being in order to fit within asymmetrical constraints. In tandem fashion, perhaps her malnourished twin sister had to collapse her physical being in order to fit the uterine confines. It is also plausible that her twin sister enacted in the physical realm a constrictive, unenlivening psychical process that jeopardized them both.

Melinda began to describe a lifelong inner desperation to internalize all there was around her, which in early childhood she channelled into intellectual domains. She stated that she always knew what she wanted and worked actively to get it, akin to getting most of the nourishment available in the womb. She recounted time spent in her brother's closet as a young girl, curled up in the semidarkness reading his books. Unconsciously, Melinda would retreat to a womblike environment where she could replay her urgent need to satiate herself, and perhaps connect with the phantasy of being a singleton. Here again, we can see the translation of symmetrical experience into the highly asymmetrical mode of language and intellect, and the use of that intellect as a route back to deeper symmetry.

At this juncture, the meaning of the nagging bewilderment the analyst felt in determining and attending to Melinda's needs became clearer. The analyst recognized her anxious perplexity as an identification with Melinda's internal representation of a uterine environment that was subjectively experienced as only marginally sufficient and upon which she could not rely to meet her needs. Via projective identificatory relatedness, the analyst had become the uterine habitat that was always in jeopardy of not being adequate. The analyst, as the object of Melinda's relatedness, also became the subject of her experience.

A painful childhood memory of standing in a room with a book in her hands, waiting "futilely" for her parents to respond to an accomplishment of which she felt proud, and turning away with the recognition that she would have to provide a response for herself also took on new meaning as we explored this material. While the theme of not being adequately acknowledged was pervasive throughout Melinda's childhood, this screen memory, at its most basic level, codified her *fetal* sense of having to assure her own survival. The symbolic connection between Melinda's intellect and her psychological needs and her choice of the word "futilely" were keys to this layer of meaning. At the core of her insecurity was Melinda's experience of waiting "fetally," not just "futilely," for her environment to provide. As Melinda was raised within a family far beyond the edges of physical or psychological survival, family dynamics alone, conscious or unconscious, could not account well for the primitiveness or tenacity of this anxiety. The threat to her survival at the level at which it originally existed had direct import that was expressed through her bodily symptoms and her fear-laden reaction to it. The signature motif for Melinda's life emanated from her prenatal experience. Only through her own determination and persistence could she feel assured that she was a living being and would survive.

Vestiges of a patient's experience within the womb can be discerned in kinesthetic or perceptual sensations; in language, metaphor, or eidetic imagery; in behavior; or in qualities of the analytic relationship or process that may be nebulous or obscure. In relatively intact individuals, such as Jill and Melinda, intrauterine motifs usually are intermingled with themes from later development and internally experienced. In less highly organized individuals, prenatal dynamics are more apt to be enacted in the world. In the context of severe disturbance, relics of fetal psychic life may be openly expressed, pervasive, and comparatively untempered by later experiences. One schizophrenic patient described himself as "what happens when a bad sperm meets a bad egg." Another psychotic man felt that he was first psychically injured when the obstetrician "tore him from his placenta." These psychotic individuals lived their lives locked in an experiential realm that had never been coded in conventional asymmetrical logic. They sustained a sense of self embedded in their experiences before or during birth.

The cases of Jill and Melinda also illustrate the somatic channels through which prenatal subjectivity is often expressed. In all of these patients, some physical correlate of their lives before birth was a primary clue to the archaic origins of their current subjective experience. Physical representations are inherent in the nature of fetal-maternal connections. The pregnant mother, the object towards whom fetal relatedness is directed, is represented by the uterine habitat she provides. As she is experienced through the interior of her body, physiological and relational aspects of fetal life are inextricably entangled, as are the boundaries of subjective and objective experience, and the soma and psyche of self and other.

The shared physical boundaries between fetus and mother, the primacy of physiological changes during gestation, and the blend of soma and psyche in utero make it likely that somatic channels remain close to uterine and symmetrical experience. Thus, it is plausible that many psychosomatic disturbances have prenatal roots. Skin disorders, disturbances in weight or body image, and psychological vulnerabilities around body integrity and cohesiveness seem particularly reminiscent of malignant or toxic experiences in the womb. People suffering with psychotic, psychosomatic, or borderline symptoms can seem untreatable or incomprehensibly idiosyncratic because much of their experience and communications echo a period of life that most people neither are able to access freely, nor consciously comprehend. They remain immersed in a realm of experience that does not fit the asymmetrical dimensions in which others seek understanding.

PRENATAL MOTIFS AND THE ANALYTIC SITUATION

The impressionistic nature of intrauterine life and the drastic line of demarcation between pre- and postnatal life render much of intrauterine experience indeterminable. The demands for conscious cognition that make us alive and human forge a gap between the symmetrical properties of prenatal life and the asymmetrical properties of psychoanalytic thinking and inference. Memories of fetal life that can be retrieved are often vague, obscure, and coded in ways that are no longer dominant in adult psychic life. Language, the currency of psychoanalytic interchange, is weak in its power to bridge the gap between the more symmetrical prenatal mode and the more asymmetrical postnatal mode. In Matte-Blanco's terms, language is an asymmetrical/anaclitic manifestation of emotional experience and, by definition, is formulated differently and is less inclusive than the emotion from which it arises. Thus, there remains a realm of affective experience that is not, and cannot be, captured by words. Within this realm lies antenatal experience.

Such considerations make qualities of prenatal life difficult to ascertain with conviction. The criterion against which prenatal constructions in analysis should be measured is their ability to augment clinical or theoretical meaningfulness. Their value lies in their capacity to expand, rather than to constrict, understanding, not in their correspondence to an objectively verifiable standard. In this sense, constructions about fetal life are not unlike many other analytic constructions. However, because prenatal motifs are less familiar to our conscious comprehension than are themes regarding later life, prenatal postulations can seem more speculative and inferential than other analytic postulations.

Consequently, antenatal representations in analytic material too often are presumed to be metaphorical artifacts of postnatal relatedness. Although the unraveling of postnatal relational dynamics is critical in therapy, exclusive attention to derivative modes of experience does not always address the manner in which experience is subjectively present for the individual. An assumption that prenatal subjectivity is not retrievable and perhaps is even unimportant negates the traces of fetal existence that many patients need to share and need to have recognized in order to feel understood and psychically integrated. The literal interpretation of prenatal material can have meaning that symbolic interpretation cannot encompass. The speculation that constructions about prenatal subjectivity entail is warranted by its potential to enhance analytic meaningfulness and to allow forays into realms of experience presumed inaccessible to interpretation or empathic inquiry. The risk in not venturing into the realm of intrauterine imagoes when relevant material is presented is to curtail an exploration of continuity of self that may be profoundly meaningful to a given patient and which cannot be reached via other channels of understanding.

To move into a domain where experience is ill defined and does not follow asymmetrical modes of logic or thought or conform easily to verbal articulation challenges our boundaries and sense of groundedness. The barriers that challenge presents to our appreciation of prenatal experience are compounded by the standard analytic setting, which mirrors the opposite of prenatal relatedness. Verbal interaction, physical separation, and the maintenance of boundaries parallel the asymmetrical mode that permeates adult psychic adaptation, but these qualities do not characterize prenatal life. From Sullivan's (1989) point of view, the standard defining features of the analytic frame represent the masculine side of the analytic process, while experiences of being, rather than doing, reflect the feminine. In Sullivan's language—and not surprisingly—it is the feminine principle that gives rise to the understanding of antenatal subjectivity. The intense and often unconscious affect exchange between analyst and patient, which often remains an intangible undercurrent in the analytic process, harkens back to the symmetrical unity and subject relating that connect mother and fetus. Unconscious aspects of the analytic relationship constitute a psychic umbilicus through which imprints of this early relatedness can be discerned.

The reluctance of analysts to give credence to the influence of prenatal experience on the contours of personality and the development of a therapeutic structure that is not conducive to the recreation of intrauterine experience have meaning. Analysts may harbor unconscious needs to seek distance from the psychic fragility of intrauterine existence by preserving the phantasy that wombs are safe, protected havens where one is loved, secure, and blissfully comfortable. The analytic environment may have derived its structure from the unconscious need to preserve this phantasy and to check intense pulls towards a prenatal experiential state. The dominance of a masculine orientation and the asymmetrical pulls in analytic conceptualization may have distracted our thinking and impeded our vision. If we can take a closer look, we can discern that prenatal experience offers a unique window on the realm of symmetry, on the unfolding of symmetrical into asymmetrical/anaclitic modes of being, and on the earliest experiences of subject-relating.

7

SUBJECT RELATIONS AS SEEN THROUGH PRENATAL OBSERVATION

Karen Lombardi

Within psychoanalytic developmental theory, there have been two distinct versions of development that reflect different assessments of the mental and relational capacities of infants and young children. These are not simply two versions of development, but also signify two visions of development, with different motivational systems and different developmental goals. The version of human development on which most American psychologists were raised is that of Margaret Mahler, who, in her explication of the psychological development of the human infant through processes of separation and individuation, maintains that physical and psychological births are not coordinate in time. Rather, infants are born without ego, and without the reference points to the external world that object cathexis will later provide them.

Object cathexes only gradually develop, being completely absent in the period of the first month or so, during the period that Mahler termed normal autism. In the second and third months of life, which Mahler called normal symbiosis, object cathexis is directed to the periphery of a posited merged unit of self and other, a fusion of mother and child where the infant is only vaguely aware of his own body boundaries and of the existence of an external world. As narcissistic cathexis gives way to object cathexis, the ego is born, (Mahler's hatching subphase) and the infant, in rudimentary ways, comes to distinguish the inside from the outside. With this psychological birth of the infant, at four months or so, development proceeds according to the principles of separation and individuation, which gradually accomplish a shift from the initial state of psychic nonexistence to an intermediate state of merger to an ultimate state of separation. The developmental goal in this system is psychic and pragmatic autonomy, the ability to live on one's own, through one's own experience, and to negotiate the world adaptively and independently.

An alternative version of human development is provided by Melanie Klein and overlaps with W.R.D. Fairbairn (1952) and various other members of the British Middle School. In this version, infants are born with rudimentary egos—or to state this in terms of process rather than of structure—with integrating tendencies. The early ego lacks the cohesion of the later ego, and its tendency toward integration alternates with a tendency towards disintegration, or what Klein (1946) calls "a falling into bits" (p. 4). Even in this early state, there are functions of the ego that exist from the beginnings of life, notably various means of dealing with anxiety. In the Kleinian version of developmental theory, object relations exist from the beginning of life, concomitant with the presence of ego. Like Mahler, Klein remains loyal to Freudian theory with respect to the preservation of drives as inborn instincts, hardwired in the individual. Unlike Mahler, however, drives for Klein are expressed only in relation to the object, freeing her theory from the notion of primary narcissism.

When there is object cathexis from the start, the nature of relatedness is reframed. Relatedness is no longer a secondary phenomenon tied to the recognition that a person outside of the self is the provider of drive satisfaction. Rather, relatedness is a primary phenomenon, occurring from the moment of original contact between infant and other. In this theory, the individual is simultaneously separate, in the sense of having a rudimentary functioning ego from the beginning, and related to others, at least in part-object form, from birth. It is not separation itself that is the goal of development, but psychic integration.

Improved modern empirical methods of infant observation have deeply affected theories of early development within psychoanalysis, and have particularly affected the ways in which we regard the two theoretical strains elucidated here. Since the first publication in the early 1960s of empirical studies of infancy that specifically set out to demonstrate the infant as a competent being, a proliferation of observational data (e.g., Stern, 1985) suggests that infants are much more competent, and more integrated from a psychic point of view than previously believed. Such data tend to refute such theoretical constructs as normal autism and normal symbiosis, and support such constructs as integrating tendencies present from birth.

Although such findings have been widely accepted, theory has not incorporated these concepts well. Theorists continue to speak of separation, for example, as if it were the major developmental task, despite the fact that there is no evidence for seeing merger as the basic relational state out of which the individual must emerge. In fact, cross-cultural studies (Roland, 1988) have augmented the argument that separation is not the sine qua non of development, by showing the developmental progression toward individuation to be a cultural artifact rather than a universal striving. Thus, in contrast to American culture, some cultures presume that psychological autonomy is the fundamental human state, and a dependent orientation must be actively cultivated. In our thinking, however, neither separation nor merger are solely the primary psychological state; rather, both exist from the earliest beginnings of life in dialectical relationship to each other. It is the dialectical correspondence, rather than its contents, that is inherently human.

Modern technology has afforded us the opportunity to observe the beginnings of life in ways that were unimaginable previously. The rather remarkable data gathered by Piontelli (1992) and others that observe intrauterine life in vivo through sonogram techniques further suggest that object relations may begin not with hatching as Mahler posited, nor even at birth as Klein asserted, but in utero. Piontelli's work with singletons and twins, both in utero and in follow-ups after birth suggest that certain predispositions for relatedness may exist at some point in prenatal development. Her fascinating studies of the parents of these fetuses during pregnancy and over lengthy follow-ups of parents and children in the first months and years after birth suggest that these capacities for relatedness tend to demonstrate continuity of experience pre- and postnatally. This is particularly true when phantasies of the parents converge and underscore the nature of pre- and postnatal experiences.

Piontelli's medium, the sonogram, was concrete, yielding observable data that could be codified in terms of fetal motility (in particular, hiccups, swallowing, micturition, breathing, and what are characterized as purposeful actions, such as change in position, thumb-sucking, manipulation of the umbilical cord). Some of the questions that Piontelli asks of her data, such as, "Do the mother's emotions affect the fetus?" are also concrete. For example, she looks to the possibility of toxic effects of maternal anxiety and maternal psychosis on the biochemistry of the womb environment.

While this line of investigation is interesting on its own, we are more compelled by the inferential possibilities of parental phantasies of the fetus, and the personification of the fetus as it seems to relate to projective and introjective processes of the parents. Glimpses into the ways in which parents attribute psychic life to the baby shed light on, perhaps, the earliest relations between self and other/subject and object. The parents' animation of the shadows on the sonogram screen provided glimpses into their developing psychic identifications with their idea of their baby, and into the ways in which parents and fetus already were interacting psychically with each other.

To further this discussion, brief overviews of three of Piontelli's clinical examples are presented: Giulia, whom we will discuss in terms of merger themes; Pina, whom we will discuss in terms of the dangers of detachment; and Alice and Luca, fraternal twins who embody the simultaneity of separateness and relatedness.

Giulia

On first meeting Giula's mother when she was thirteen weeks pregnant, Piontelli describes her as tall, enormous in her maternity dress, heavily made-up, fleshy lipped, whorish in a caricatured way, "like a character out of a Fellini film" (p. 41). On subsequent meetings, she lost this Felliniesque sensuality, looking instead pale and washed out. Quite consistently throughout the ultrasonographic observation, Giulia was observed by Piontelli and other personnel in the act of frequently opening and closing her mouth, sucking her tongue and her thumb, licking her hands as well as the placenta and umbilical cord, and placing her hands between her legs.

After her sex was identified, at the thirtieth week, the mother's comments were of concerned identification with the fetus: "I used to suck my tongue too when I was a child. . . . I went on doing it 'til I was at least five" (p. 46). The father's comments tended to be both defensively distant and disparaging, "Once they are out . . . they are really horrible . . . until they are at least six to seven months old they look terrible" (46) and "How disgusting!" (p. 49). At the thirty-fifth week, the mother began to worry that the baby was too big and would "remain stuck inside" (p. 48), a reflection of her worries about her own weight ("I am too fat . . . she will never come out") (p. 50). The delivery, which Piontelli attended, sounded quite ghastly, like something out of a Fellini film itself, with the mother exhausted, her mood moving from fear to terror, and the delivery attendants literally lying on her stomach, pushing with their knees and feet to get the baby to come down. In the midst of this barbaric scene, Giulia emerged seemingly unperturbed, not crying unless poked at, and returning quickly to a calm and placid state.

Two days postpartum, mother and child were visited in the hospital. Giulia demonstrated a certain continuity of behavior from inside the uterus to the outside world, as well as certain differences. She continued to suck her own tongue, but seemed less interested in sucking at the breast. Rather, she would lick the breast when her mother offered it to her, and lick her own hand quite vigorously, as she was observed to do in the womb. Her interest in licking remained, but her interest in food was negligible during this visit. Her mother's comments about her reflect themes of merger and death:

> She didn't want to come out from the womb . . . she liked it too much in there . . . I was scared . . . I was afraid she was never going to come out . . . I felt trapped . . . I was afraid I was never going to make it . . . we would have both died . . . It is difficult to get used to all this . . . she was inside before . . . now suddenly she is outside . . . I was afraid she would be born small because I was on a diet . . . just think of it? (pp. 58–9)

Given this mother's own concerns with merger, which interacted with eating and body image, it is not surprising that incorporative themes began to dominate Giulia's life. On follow-up visits until the age of three, the home was described as chaotic and "like a gargantuan cellar," with copious amounts of food everywhere. Giulia was described as a voracious baby, whose appetite for food was matched in all modalities; looking, licking, hearing, touching, rocking. Mother's description of Giulia's incorporative pleasures, as she drew attention to Giulia's wild reaction to the sound of her grandfather's voice was, "She is really a little whore . . . she is mad about men" (p. 61). This atmosphere of indiscriminate sensuality and indulgence was fostered by the mother and grandmother, who centered their own "sensuous and wandering" attentions on Giulia's activities within the confines of "the narrow space of her grandmother's home" where, according to the mother, Guilia could be "fed and cuddled like a baby" (p. 62–3).

Interestingly, Piontelli saw Giulia in twice-weekly psychotherapy after the birth of her brother when she was three. Giulia's reaction to his birth was to close herself up in her room and to sleep, to cling to her mother, and to refuse to see visitors. We see this reaction less in terms of jealousy or anxiety about being displaced by her brother than in terms of her rather remarkable identification with her mother. Her play in the first session focused on being shut in, shut up, having no opening, not being able to come out, and a running commentary of observations on what is inside and what is outside, which find remarkable parallel in her mother's anxieties as they were expressed before and immediately after Guilia's birth. The description of Giulia's appearance at this first session is nearly identical to the description of the mother at Piontelli's first meeting with her: "She is quite tall and terribly fat. Her obesity is rendered even more evident by her tight purple trousers and by the glossy embroidery of her equally purple blouse that somehow gives her a rather whorish and vulgar appearance" (p. 64). At the end of the session, mother says that Giulia has been put on a diet by the doctor because her blood pressure is quite high. Mother speaks of this situation with great urgency: "alarming . . . I was so scared," and then goes on to say to Giulia, "I am sure you must be starving. I'll buy you some chips" (pp. 65–66).

Pina

Pina distinguished herself by unusually vigorous intrauterine activity, continually moving and exploring her own body and the environment of the womb. She was observed scratching her cheeks, rubbing her eyes, scratching her chest, kicking, reorienting her entire body, holding her feet with her hands, yawning, swallowing, pulling at the placenta and touching her face against it. She was seen by observers to be a most lively and active fetus, very exploratory in her movements. While observing Pina pulling at the placenta, the obstetrician remarked, "What is it doing? . . . Trying to pull the placenta towards itself . . . it's incredible what it's doing with it . . . it's the typical maneuver of manual detachment of the placenta . . . but be careful! . . . stop doing it! . . . it is dangerous you know . . . you could be detaching it!" (p. 90). A few days later, the mother began to bleed and an initial detachment of the placenta was noted. She was put on bed rest and given tocolytic drugs. Interestingly, on subsequent sonograms this previously very active fetus stopped moving and was observed to be curled up in a corner of the womb, basically immobile. This immobility continued well past the course of drugs she was given, to the point where she remained in the transverse position and a cesarean delivery was performed. Piontelli reports, "Apparently Dr. S. had considerable difficulty in pulling her out of the womb and one of her feet, due to the malposition in utero, had to be put in plaster. Dr. S. was struck by the fact that Pina cried at first, but then seemed greatly relieved to be out, and described her as a 'vivacious and alert child.'"

In follow-up visits, Pina is described as an alert, precocious baby whose alertness had a certain tense or paranoid quality while in the house, but not while outside, where she appeared much more relaxed and less tensely vigilant. Mother said of the infant Pina: "Constriction and being inside equal danger for her . . . she would like to live like a gypsy in the street" (p. 97). While an active explorer of her environment, Pina showed a fear of falling, manifested by screams at bath time and fears of being walked up or down the stairs. This fear of falling may be understood as well in the Winnicottian sense of not being held psychically.

At three, when mother was again pregnant and about to give birth, Piontelli visited them and Pina drew her a picture of "an unlucky egg . . . it is going to be washed away by the waves of the sea . . . these are a lot of other eggs . . . no danger for them . . . they are lucky . . . they firmly planted inside the ground" (p. 103). Mother interpreted that they went to the sea that summer and Pina was first frightened by the waves; that she spent the summer happily with her grandmother, along with her parents, having fun weeding and digging and picking in the fields. Pina then showed some scratches on her arm, saying "Look, I did these when I was out in the fields . . . they left a scar . . . wounds always leave a deep scar" (p. 103).

Piontelli concludes: "Although Pina's mother had not explicitly told Pina about her near miscarriage, Pina seems to show tacit awareness of the danger she had been subjected to, and has a persisting tendency towards vigorous activity, almost hyperactivity, accompanied or followed by fear of disaster or tragedy" (p. 107). This case description suggests that this tendency of Pina's is not only rooted in the prenatal experience of near abortion and her mother's anxiety and concern for their endangered relationship, but in the continued concern about whether she can be held sufficiently to keep her from danger. The mother, herself, having migrated north from a little Calabrian village where life was more cooperative and less isolated, had her own anxieties about danger of detachment. She very strongly communicated her own sense of ease when she was outside, in the open countryside, in the presence of her own mother, an ease which she did not feel cooped up in her house in the city. Pina's claustrophobia and fear of detachment may be seen not only as referring to her prenatal experience of placental detachment, but also to her articulation of her relationship with her mother who was ripped away from the rootedness of her ancestral vilage and living a more isolated and internal northern life. Their mutual experience of being ripped away constitutes a symmetrical experience.

Alice and Luca

Alice and Luca's mother's stated on the way to her first sonogram study: "Babies are all different . . . you can see it from the start . . . I don't see why fetuses shouldn't be different too . . . even with identical twins, I am sure there are some differences . . . we all have different selves" (p. 128–9), which underscores our view that the psychic relations of the parents, conscious and unconscious, help shape the earliest interactions, even phantasied interactions, between parent and child.

These babies, fraternal twins, were observed to be quite different from each other from their first ultrasounds at twenty weeks. Luca, the boy, was both smaller and more active than Alice, the girl. Most remarkable here, as with all of Piontelli's twin observations, was the opportunity to observe physical interactions between fetuses. Luca, in his activity, characteristically would reach out through the dividing membrane to stroke Alice's cheek, to which she would respond by moving in closer to him, head to head or cheek to cheek. The observers nicknamed them "the kind twins" for their gentle movement toward each other and their tendency to be in close contact.

What we find most notable throughout the prenatal studies of Alice and Luca is their parents' sensitive observations concerning their individuality, as well as their identification with them. For example, as the physician described Luca's motor activity, alternatively touching his own face and the uterine wall, the father commented, "Perhaps it can feel the difference . . . this is me, this is not me . . . me . . . not me" (p. 131). When the physician described Luca articulating the movement of each digit, mother remarked smiling, "My husband likes playing the piano" (p. 132). As mother commented on the stroking between the fetuses, the father mused,

> They seem to cuddle up together . . . look how he strokes her. I am quite convinced that they know there is another person in there . . . that they feel boundaries . . . and have a sense of being themselves . . . other people perhaps could argue that she is not aware that his movement comes from outside herself . . . that they're too self-centered and absorbed to realize the existence of something and someone outside themselves . . . but these images are pretty convincing . . . of course, I cannot prove it, but they seem to me to be already two very separate beings, each with its own clear identity." (p. 134)

In follow-up visits, Luca continued to be more active than Alice, both in terms of psychomotor exploration and in terms of various indications of interest in the outside world: walking, talking, looking at pictures, drawing. Alice, more placid and seemingly less intelligent, followed Luca by a few months, and a bit less proficiently. As Luca put it during play with toy cars: "They run together . . . next to each other . . . but the small car will get there first in the end . . . it is lighter, faster" (p. 144). The twins continued to be well related to each other, and their interactions marked a characteristic gentleness. At about one year old, their favorite game was to hide on either side of a curtain with Alice reaching out with her head, stroking each other as they did in the womb. The parents continued to value the differences they perceived in each child, and were themselves both quite gentle and appreciative of individuality.

INTEGRATION, DIFFERENTIATION, AND
THE SYNTHESIS OF EXPERIENCE

These remarkable ultrasonographic observations provide data for interesting speculations about the continuity of experience pre- and postnatally, and raise questions about the nature of psychic organization and capacities for relatedness in the human infant. The sense of emergent self and the domain of emergent relatedness as described by Stern (1985) in the first month or two of life, or in Anzieu's (1989) formulation of the bodily pre-ego of the neonate, which is equipped with a disposition to integrate sensory data, and a tendency to move toward objects and develop ways of being with them, can be observed in some nascent form in utero. The demarcation between internal and external, which is the prototype for the sense of self and other and for both experiences of relatedness and later symbolic experience, may be laid down not during the hatching phase or at birth, but in utero. Here, within the uterine environment, rudimentary sensory experience of inside and outside occur between self and other, establishing and reflecting templates for characteristics of temperament, self-organization, and relational patterns. What traditionally has been considered inside contains experiences of both inside and outside. Margins between self and other can be tested through contact with the uterine wall, or through contact with separate membranes within the uterine space which, in turn, may contain an other developing alongside the self.

Also striking from a psychical perspective is the function of sonographic techniques for eliciting both conscious attitudes and unconscious phantasies of parent in relation to their babies. The continuity of development observed in Piontelli's subjects may be understood in terms of those unconscious phantasies and feelings relating parent and children before birth. Shared unconscious qualities between parent and child come to comprise their mutual subjectivity, such that each individual partakes in and fashions the other's subjective experience. What appears to be individual subjectivity is, more accurately, jointly created and jointly experienced, existing in the psychic space of their unconscious relationship. The nature of these phantasies and attitudes continues to be articulated in the growing relationship between parents and child throughout early life, and underscores or mitigates the experience, be it perilous or secure, of life in the womb, fostering or inhibiting integrating tendencies of the individual.

The new analytic explorations into the realm of fetal subjectivity also promote reconsideration of conventionally held distinctions between inner and outer realities and self and other experience. The Mahlerian view of reality is limited by its positivistic foundations, whereby reality is construed in absolutes and unidirectional terms. Adaptation to the demands of the external world becomes focal in the move from infancy to childhood, and the process of separation and individuation becomes increasingly intertwined with the adaptive requirement exerted by reality. The Kleinian view of the infant's relationship to the world permits a psychic realm between internal and external reality in which symbolization and personal meaning can be formulated. Neither phantasy nor external reality is absolute. External reality is not just objective and psychic reality is not just subjective; rather, both are versions of reality. Even when perceived as external, reality is experienced subjectively, constructed in a subject-subject matrix. In Piontelli's case studies, what was in the parents' psyches was also in the fetus's behavior; how the fetus behaved was in the parents' psyches; and what the fetus experienced (which we can only infer) seemed to be expressed behaviorally.

As with internal and external reality, we view self and other distinctions as experienced, not given or perceived; they are constructed experientially, and synergistically through their relationship to their opposite. In contrast to models that see identity formation as the move toward autonomy or individuality, we posit a dialectical flow between integration and disintegration as the goal of development. Development proceeds through the splitting and the integration of self and object experience, through dialectical movement between differentiation and dedifferentiation. In this latter view, the goal of maturity is the flexibility to move bidirectionally between states of differentiation and states of dedifferentiation.

Identity formation, then, is not based on difference, on the gradual disentangling of self and other, as much as it is based on the continual interplay between experiences of sameness and experiences of difference. The gradual synthesis of experiences of inside and outside, subject and object, self and other is accompanied, in dialectical form, by their gradual extrication. At one pole of this dialectic is autonomy and individuality and, at the other, is merger and connectedness. The process of merging and connecting is not only the coming together of disparate, discrete entities, but also, and perhaps simultaneously, the experiencing of a dedifferentiated embeddedness in which all things exist in unpotentiated form. Individuation is not just the detachment of self from other, but the experience of self as distinct from other even in the context of connection. Piontelli's parents and babies, for example, did not just find the separateness in each other over time, but they also found their unity; they engaged with each other in a subjective mode.

Movement toward and away from wholeness, toward and away from immersion in mutually subjective and symmetrical experience and, correspondingly, toward and away from asymmetry and object-relatedness is in the essence of the human condition. The capacity for a distinct sense of self coexists with the capacity for an experience of unity and homogeneity. The development of individual identity lies not in the predetermined superiority of psychic autonomy, but in the potentiation of subjective and objective experience and in the flexibility to shift between these experiential modes.

8

MOTHER AS OBJECT, MOTHER AS SUBJECT

Karen Lombardi

Different accounts of normal development of the individual infant rest on two divergent psychoanalytic frameworks, those of one-person and two-person psychologies. Those accounts of normal infant development that focus on the movement from merger and symbiosis to individuation are based on one-person psychologies, which rest on the various premises of drive theory. Most relevant to developmental theory is the premise that babies are born into the world as drive-dominated organisms, and that only gradually do they come to discriminate, on both purely perceptual and on psychological bases, that they are separate from their environmental surround. Given this premise, individuation comes to be the hallmark of personal development. Two-person psychologies, on the other hand, tend to stress aspects of integrity in the baby from the beginning and to consider the baby's capacity for rudimentary integrative functioning on both perceptual and psychological levels. The developmental focus, then, is not on separation and individuation, but on object-relating and connectedness. Since much of the recent work in two-person psychology tends to focus on adult psychology and on the psychoanalytic treatment process, the logical implications for an account of the course of normal development are often missed, and those who embrace two-person psychologies often continue to regard merger and symbiosis as normal developmental markers.

The other focus of this argument is on the adult in the baby-adult dyad, who in most (but not all) cases is the mother. Concepts of the feminine and the maternal, colored as they have been by the lens of drive theory, have not been articulated by internally consistent versions of two-person psychologies. The very arguments that have been made to lift concepts of the feminine and the maternal out of drive theory and into relational models have been mired in essentialist versions of the feminine and the maternal, in which women are seen in some way naturally to excel in the merger and symbiosis supposedly characteristic of mother-child relations. The need to counteract the more traditional patriarchal views of women has elevated the very concepts that most belong to instinct theory and one-person psychologies. Consonance with the two person frameworks of relational models requires more than a revisionist version of the unity between mother and child. It requires that the separateness and integrity inherent in mother and in child and the search for relatedness within that context be considered.

Cultures that value individualism, in the material sense as well as the symbolic sense, place more value on the developmental concept of individuation. American culture, for example, which promotes a strike-it-rich individualistic mentality to counteract the notion that there are groups of people who suffer in the society because of social policy, generates images of rugged individualism that have both negative and positive aspects. This cultural value system is consistent with individuation as a goal of development. Valuing merger and symbiosis as a counterfoil to the negative aspects of individualism retains the linear, dichotomous model that is being criticized. Further articulations of the meaning of symbiosis and merger within the context of individuation would clarify how these concepts relate fundamentally to one-person psychologies. Returning to such basic concepts as introjection and identification, and explicating them within a relational model, helps move us in the direction of a developmental psychology that is freer of the cumbersome accommodations that are characteristic of attempts to wed object relations to ego psychology that have marked many recent efforts.

SEPARATION-INDIVIDUATION OR INTEGRATION?: MAHLERIAN AND KLEINIAN VIEWS OF HUMAN DEVELOPMENT

Although there is a widening acceptance that infants have a constructive relationship with the environmental surround at least from birth, negating Mahler's (1975) posited stage of primary narcissism, her work on separation-individuation continues to serve as an organizing framework for understanding not only human psychological development, but human nature and the nature of human relationships. Mahler's theory posited a drive towards individuation that is based on the premise that the given human relational state is that of merger or fusion with the mother. The goal of development in this system is the move to autonomy, which consists of separation from the symbiotic dual unity with the mother, and the simultaneous move from the pleasure principle to the reality principle, with consequential intrapsychic differentiation of the ego apparatuses of perception, memory, cognition, and so forth. Concepts of merger or dual unity, in this theory, are necessary precisely because the theory is based in the drive theory principle of primary narcissism. Relational experiences, rather than inhering in the experience of what it is to be human, are forced into the individual because of the press of reality and the need to move from the pleasure principle and adapt to reality. One needs merger to be pulled out of the pure primary narcissism of the autistic phase, and later, one needs the father as the representative of power and excitement in the outside world to be pulled out of merger.

In Mahlerian theory, identity formation is both genderized and seen in terms of the goal of autonomy or individuality. In the present view, the goal of development is not individuation and autonomy, but integration. In the one case, the developmental move is from merger to separation-individuation, which results in mature autonomy; in the other the move is from the splitting of self and object experience to the integration of self and object experience, forming a dialectical interplay between differentiation and dedifferentiation. In the latter view, the goal of mature development is the flexibility to move from states of differentiation to states of dedifferentiation and back. Although there have been excellent attempts to recast Mahlerian theory into a more object-relational framework (Carstairs, 1992) or into an attachment paradigm (Lyons-Ruth, 1991), Kleinian theory and the work of the British Middle School theorists are far more suited to viewing development and the construction of identity in terms of integration, rather than differentiation.

The focus of Mahlerian theory is on difference and on those for whom difference is seen as really possible. In Mahler's theory, boys have an easier time during rapprochement, partly because of their awareness of their gender difference from their mother, while girls have a harder—or at least a more sober and de-pressed—time of it because of their recognition that they are the same as their mothers. Mahler frames this sameness in terms of lack; both mother and girl-child lack penises, and the girl child comes to resent the mother for this state of affairs. Mature identity formation is based on autonomy, and autonomy is based on the process of separation from the mother and individuation of the self. Difference facilitates autonomy.

The Kleinian exposition of identity formation is based on introjective and projective processes, where there is a constant interplay between aspects of self-experience and aspects of object-experience, with each being projected out and introjected, reprojected, and reintrojected. Identity formation, then, is not based on experiences of difference, on the gradual disentangling of self and other, as much as it is based on the continual interplay between experiences of fusion or identity and experiences of separateness and differentiation. Gradual integrations of what initially is projected out allow for fuller and richer experiences of the self as disentangled from the other at the same time that the self maintains an identity with the other. In Kleinian theory, the introjections upon which identity is based are less gender focused than in Mahlerian theory. The object contains both good and bad and both masculine and feminine attributes, including male and female body parts. The one who contains the penis, then (with a nod to Freud), or the one who contains the phallus (with a nod to Lacan), may be the mother, just as the one who contains the breast (good or bad) may be the father.

THE PROBLEM OF THE RELATIONSHIP TO REALITY: DIFFERING VIEWS OF REALITY AND PHANTASY

One of the limitations of Mahlerian theory is in its conception of and relationship to reality. Reality is construed in absolutes or positivist terms; it is given, not constructed, and the infant, especially, exists in oppositional tension to the demands of reality, which are seen to disturb psychic equilibrium and to thwart the pleasure-seeking instinctual drives of the infant. Adaptation to the demands of the external world becomes focal in the move from infancy to childhood, and the process of separation and individuation becomes increasingly intertwined with the adaptive requirements exerted by reality. On the one hand, Mahler has been given credit for humanizing drive theory, because she brings in the effects of actual parenting and other aspects of the environmental surround on the developing individual. At the same time, this orientation to reality tends to overvalue an external world that is seen as a given, and people who have attempted to revise Mahler to fit more progressive views (e.g., Chodorow, 1978, 1989) tend also to propose solutions in the external world, concretizing both the source and the solution.

In the Kleinian view, reality and phantasy are not counterposed, nor are instinct and desire seen as coming in opposition to reality. Rather, phantasy is in itself a form of psychic reality; in the same way, external reality is not objective or absolute, but only one form of reality. The Kleinian view lends itself more readily to such a constructivist concept of reality, since it is in the interplay between inner psychic reality and external reality that symbol formation takes place, and it is in the interplay between internal and external realities that personal meaning is constructed. In this view, the development of individual identity is more potentiation than predetermination as all is possible, but only as it is articulated within the continual dialectic between internal and external experience.

RELATIONAL FEMINISM AND MAHLERIAN DEVELOPMENTAL THEORY

Recently, there have been many interesting attempts to lift concepts of the feminine and the maternal out of drive theory and into relational models of development and identity formation. Brief reference will be made to some of those more important attempts, especially as they relate to implications for developmental theory. Each of these works take issue with Mahlerian ideas at the same time that Mahlerian concepts continue to be central to their way of thinking.

Self-in-relation theory (Jordan, et al., 1991) suggests that fusion or merger is a result of distortion in caretaking, which is similar to Stern's (1985) argument that these experiences pertain more to certain kinds of relatedness than to normal developmental stages. Differentiation is seen as coexisting with fusion or merger and is described in terms of varying qualities of intimate attachment. Nevertheless, these theorists return to gender differences, where their real interests seem to lie, and conclude that girls are better at the things the authors value (connectedness, concern, empathy, and so on). The theorists do understand important dimensions of the cultural context, but keep reverting to essentialist or natural arguments regarding the superiority of women's connectedness, especially in the developmental context of the mother-daughter relationship.

Chodorow (1989) attempts to revise the Mahlerian view of differentiation by placing it within a relational context. She accepts Mahler's premise that we move from symbiotic unity to differentiation, but focuses on that differentiation as a means of relating to the mother or primary caretaker. She attempts to position separation-individuation within a relational field by refocusing the concept: "differentiation is not synonymous with difference or separateness" (p. 101). However, at the same time that she defines herself as relational, she continues to use concepts that belong to one-person psychology in accepting the premise that infants are born with a narcissistic relation to reality, and that the predominant experience in infancy is that of merger with the world in general, and with the mother or caretaker in particular.

Differentiation, then, by necessity remains a central premise, as it is the means by which the individual comes to perceive him/herself as separate from the other. So Chodorow, espousing a relational orientation, continues to view narcissism and a narcissistic relation to reality as a developmental given. Not only is this concept incongruent with relational theory, but there is some evidence from current infant research that the experience of separateness is hardwired from birth and little evidence that narcissism or symbiosis are inborn givens.

Chodorow views differentiation not simply as separateness, but as a particular experience. She simultaneously continues to see merger problems as influenced by gender in some generic sense: "Feelings of inadequate separateness, the fear of merger, are indeed issues for women, because of the ongoing sense of oneness and primary identification with our mothers (and children)" (p. 108). So, for women and girls, there remains an imbalance between merger and differentiation on the basis of gender differences, creating problems with merger. Chodorow's solution is societal; in calling for fathers to exercise maternal roles, children will have more "separateness" with which to identify.[1]

---

[1] Chodorow, in a recent (1996) paper that criticizes the causal determinism of structural developmental theory and attempts to reconcile developmental theory with the contemporary relational clinical enterprise, has come to a view that seems closer to my own. She says ". . . processual conceptions of childhood that focus on human capacities to create personal and intersubjective meanings virtually from birth, rather than theories centered on developmental stages, lines, structure formation, or tasks, points us to a more promising understanding of psychic functioning throughout life." (p. 49)

More explicitly aligned with two-person psychology, Benjamin (1988) places mothers and babies within an interactional paradigm, based on the concept of mutual recognition. She explicitly criticizes Mahler's notion of symbiotic unity and the separation-individuation paradigm, but then continues to speak from within it, and particularly of the gender-focused accounts it presents. Her account of the child's experience is that both separation and desire are joined in the father, whereas mothers' functions are more of the soothing, holding, and containing types. She presents a particular version of the rapprochement subphase which is characterized by identificatory love. Identificatory love arises in relation to the father and represents both a defensive attempt to defeat the regressive or symbiotic pulls of the mother and an identification with the father and the power and desire he represents as an agent of the outside world. Before rapprochement, loving someone as an object is already well established—the example that Benjamin provides is, "I love you—you bring me food." But loving someone as a subject first occurs in rapprochement in relation to the father. This account sounds identical to Mahler's, where the father is needed to pull the child out of the symbiotic orbit with the mother and into the excitement and activity of the external world. Benjamin's explication, however, (including the penis envy that Mahler et al. (1975), and Roiphe and Galenson (1971) presumably observed in eighteen-month-old girls) is social rather than biological.

Separation-individuation remains a hallmark of development, but the gender articulations are not biological; rather, they are social and subject to reconstruction. Benjamin criticizes the polarities of maternal (fusion and symbiosis) and paternal (autonomy and individuality) constructs and the necessity, within the Oedipal model, of differentiating male and female into irreconcilable difference and denial of identification with the opposite sex. Her appreciation that children use cross-sex identifications to formulate parts of their own selves, and that love objects embody multiple possibilities of gender, sameness, and difference do not belie her statement that the girl has a "developmental need to identify with the father" (1991, p. 277), gendering what she wishes not to gender. Without any alternative theory to account for how cross-gender identification might be made, she is left with an interesting critique that has less power and clarity than it might.

THE SENTIMENTALIZATION OF THE MATERNAL

Concepts of the feminine and the maternal within the mother-child dyad tend to portray the mother in two primary ways: (1) as serving soothing functions and posing as an "auxiliary ego," roles that are consistent with ego psychology and with Mahler's view of the role of the mother during the narcissistic stage of development; and (2) as performing containing, receptive, and responsive functions, more consistent with object-relational Kleinians and British Middle School theorists, such as Winnicott and Bion, and with American intersubjectivitists. Even those who address maternal functions without reference to gender or biology (e.g., Schwartz, 1993) speak primarily in terms of regulatory and security functions, where (m)other is viewed as attuning to the needs of the infant and functioning responsively. These conceptions of maternal functions, although tending toward thinking in terms of interaction matrices, continue to cast the mother in the role of the object in the mother-child dyad, and not the subject. To take up Benjamin's argument, the mother, cast as responsive container and attuner, remains an object, and not a subject, in the mother-child dyad. Recasting the mother as subject requires that we conceive of maternal desires that function within the mother-child relationship, facilitating (and in other ways profoundly affecting) the outcome of the relationship.

The value to both the infant and to the mother of the mother-as-subject is addressed by Likierman (1988) and by other contemporary British analysts (e.g., Alvarez, 1988). While Likierman acknowledges the importance of receptivity, responsivity, and containment as facilitators of psychic integration, she feels that an emphasis on these functions precludes another, equally important function. This function she characterizes in terms of the mother transmitting to the infant the psychical quality of her *own* feelings, which include the need for the other and the need to have her own feelings received by the other. Likierman posits two equally important aspects of maternal unconscious interaction with the infant that she views in terms of transference. The first she calls reverie, a Bionian term that includes receptivity, responsivity, and containment of the infant's experience, and a feeding back of that experience in a digested or modified form. The second she calls maternal transference proper, or positive projective identification, through which the mother transmits to the infant the psychical qualities of her *own* feelings (as opposed to what are perceived to be the infant's feelings). Here is the mother as subject that Benjamin seeks, as well as the concept of mutuality and difference from the very beginning of relatedness, which ultimately leads to mutual recognition as well as to introjection and identification. In Likierman's words, loving "is a display of feelings which has nothing to do with catering for the infant. It springs not from the infant's projections and needs, but from the mother's own deep-seated need. They are important because a mother must need her baby as a part of loving it" (p. 31).

Loving hardly seems to be a controversial concept. However, Likierman is making a revolutionary point in psychoanalytic theory: she is positing that mothers have needs of their own to be received, recognized, and expressed, and that these needs, in and of themselves, not only are not harmful, but also are necessary to psychic formation. When only maternal receptive functions are stressed, a sentimental view of the mother-child relationship is put forth that creates two falsifications: first, that of a sanitized mother who is idealized as the pure altruist; and second, that of an infant who "needs pure altruism, and does not benefit from intrusions into its psyche of a positive kind" (p. 31).

Likierman is suggesting that such intrusions, which have to do with love and desire and which also establish the mother as having her own subjectivity, are necessary for real object relatedness and eventual mutuality. They establish the experience of being the object of need, rather than only needy. Both partners in the dyad then develop a deepening capacity to experience themselves both as subject and as object, and, at least as importantly, come to have within themselves the capacity to move from subjective to objective experience and back again. Such a view of the normal or average maternal relationship has clear implications for clinical theory, because it suggests that the customary object-relational focus on receptive functions of the analyst should be balanced by a recognition of both the inevitability and the value of putting something of yourself into the relationship with the other.

The cultural construction of the maternal in American culture has gone a long way toward promoting the sentimentalization of motherhood. Recent anthropological observations offered by Schepper-Hughes (1992) suggest that naturalist accounts of maternal bonding (Klaus and Kennell, 1976), maternal thinking, and women's different voice, as characterized by an inclination to define themselves in empathic relation to others (e.g., Gilligan, 1982; Chodorow, 1978; Jordan et al., 1991) are themselves severely flawed, being simply cultural constructions themselves. Schepper-Hughes' subject was mother-infant relatedness within an impoverished urban enclave in Brazil. The material conditions that apply to women of this culture are those of scarcity. One-third to one-half of babies born in this subculture do not survive the first year. Most die of malnutrition and diarrhea/dehydration; emotional neglect accompanies biological deprivation. The high expectancy of death produces patterns of nurturing that Schepper-Hughes reported as differentiating those infants thought of as thrivers or keepers from those thought of as already wanting to die. The babies perceived as thrivers and keepers are nurtured, whereas those babies perceived as languishers are allowed to die of neglect. The languishing babies are seen as lacking the will to live, of having no gusto for life, of being too pliable, undemanding, or lazy, of lacking the resistance needed to survive in the world, and of wanting to die. Once dead, these babies are thought of as angels who have returned to God. They are not mourned in the ways that the more culturally privileged might mourn the loss of a baby or of a pregnancy. The death is unregretted in the sense that the baby is seen as having been spared a life of hardship for which he or she was not equipped. Folk wisdom discourages grieving for these babies (but not for older children, or other relatives) because of the belief that a mother's tears will impede the journey of the baby into the next world. Infants are thought to have no form, no history, and no capacity to relate; the baby is not yet personified, and so there is not yet anything to have lost.

In our culture, particularly among those privileged by material comforts and education, babies are enlivened from the moment of conception with our own phantasies, our own affects, and our own privileged lives. These particular Brazilian babies are deadened, both by their mothers' hardship and despair and by their mothers' difficulties supplying them, in both material and psychic senses, with resources that are too scarce to suffice. Only those newcomers who make their presence most felt and those in the family group who have already proven their survival capacity are likely to receive some form of lively identification. The infants who survive in this culture of scarcity are those who are most impervious, not only to malnutrition and disease, but also to projective identification around issues of scarcity, survival, and death.

Schepper-Hughes compares what she calls condemned-child syndrome to various forms of voodoo death, where a sorcerized individual is put to death symbolically by the will of the group, and then, through suggestibility, languishes and dies. She states that, for these babies, suggestibility is irrelevant (that is, they die of malnutrition and dehydration, not psychic manipulation), at the same time that she very poignantly describes a baby whom she rescues from a mother who had "let go" of the child because she was convinced that the child would die. While the mother agreed to give him up to Schepper-Hughes (she was not committed to his death), other mothers laughed at her for her experiment, saying that this was a lifeless baby, without fight, and that it was wrong to fight with death. Implicit in this culture is that the initiative for life must come from the baby.

Schepper-Hughes found the baby resisting her rescue, refusing to eat, wailing whenever anyone approached him or handled him, and finally, as he began to gain weight in spite of himself, demonstrating his ambivalence by spitting his food in her face. This seems more than simply the residue of malnutrition, but the enactment of his own internalized identification with languishment and death and, eventually, as he became stronger physically, his attempt to maintain that identificatory position. This child, when returned to his mother, not only survived, but went on to be her favorite child, her "arms and legs," the one who survived despite her indifference to him. Interestingly, in a photograph of him as a teenager with his mother and younger brother, his face is nearly identical to hers. He ends up murdered in a lovers' quarrel, and his mother, who nearly totally neglected him years before and who probably would not have mourned him if he had died then, nearly died of grief herself.

Within this culture, the object relations that characterize early mother-child experiences are more readily described in terms of the distance and estrangement of the schizoid mode than in terms of fusion, merger, or empathy. More positive and life-affirming experiences of attachment are built slowly and cautiously, once the child has demonstrated qualities of a keeper. The assumption that early experiences of merger are what is natural and essential to the feminine and maternal is presumptuous without reference to both the culture and the individual intrapsychic context. It is fairer and more accurate to speak not of the natural unity of mother and child, nor of mother as object, containing the projections of the child, but of the heterogeneity of identity and identifications within the mother herself which are simultaneously separate from and connected to the child. The child, then, does not move naturally from an undifferentiated matrix with the mother to a separate and individuated autonomous self any more than the mother serves merely as an object from which to separate, rather than a subject with whom to engage. The elaboration of the relationship between mother and child thus may be seen in terms of a continual interplay between separation and connection, and differentiation and dedifferentiation, in the integration of self and experience.

9

INTIMATE SUBJECTS

Naomi Rucker

The experience of intimacy is attributed most readily to relationships between spouses, partners, and lovers, yet intimacy has many faces. Parents and children, good friends, and patient-analyst pairs, for example, also can feel intimate. The common parlance of psychology uses terms such as building or creating intimacy, with the implication that the establishment of intimacy necessitates long, hard work and is a gradual evolving process. Yet, there also are occasions in life when intimacy can be experienced in a momentary contact with a relative stranger in which both parties instantly and intuitively know something deep, meaningful, and connecting about each other.

The experience of love-at-first-sight is a prototype of this latter experience. Other examples of such intimacy can be found in the closeness and familiarity some new mothers describe feeling with their newly born infants, or the feeling that can exist between two people who feel close despite long periods of absence from one another with little or no contact. None of these situations requires a lengthy period of interpersonal exchange, the ongoing exposure and sharing of mutual vulnerabilities, a full appreciation of each other's personality or the like. Each is based, instead, on some rather indefinable intuition about the quality of the connection each person has or could have with the other.

An argument could be made that these immediate experiences of closeness are not true intimacy, but rather are illusory or transferential feelings. Perhaps. Feelings of instantaneous closeness may be of a wholly different ilk than intimacy as it is generally construed. Alternately, both experiences of instantaneous connection and gradually evolving closeness may be only different dimensions of intimate processes.

The latter view carries greater potential for the meaningful elaboration of unconscious relational processes than the former. Contemplation of spontaneous, intuitive feelings of intimacy may reveal processes of unconscious relatedness in the intimate realm that cannot be understood if they are not recognized as a form of intimate expression. In this chapter, experiences of instantaneous connection and closeness, such as love-at-first-sight, will be called presentient intimacy. The term affiliative intimacy will refer to the more manifest, tangible, emotional connections that are generally considered as intimate.

I'M IN YOU AND YOU'RE IN ME: CONSTRUCTIONS OF SELF AND OTHER

What is it that one knows when confronted with an experience of presentient intimacy, and what does this knowing mean? The experience of being in love, whether it occurs at first sight or after many viewings often comprises a sense of being the same, having identical experiences, perspectives, inner reactions. This sameness allows us to feel the other persons' subjectivity as our own and our subjectivity as the other's. In a relationship of affiliative intimacy, where intimacy develops over time, it is easy to understand that two people come to know, understand, and appreciate each other, that two individuals come together and a relationship develops. In experiences of presentient intimacy, this is not the case. If we turn on its head the argument that intimate relationships must be built and created, we have a situation where an intimate relationship exists and two individuals come together within it; the relationship exists in some unpotentiated form prior to the literal meeting of two people. This potential relationship is the psychic space from which the actual relationship emerges, the related unconscious. Here, two unconsciouses meet and the people follow.

It feels important for us as people to experience and view ourselves as whole and consolidated, yet consolidation compromises wholeness. Consolidation implies asymmetrical boundaries and separateness, while wholeness implies symmetrical unity. We wish to be our own selves, a wish that emphasizes distinctness; we wish to see ourselves as the figure that stands apart from the ground. We do not want to be a construction of the other; rather we wish to be grounded, not (con)figured. Yet, this wish reflects a deeper knowledge that we are in fact constructed through each other and that our separateness is to some degree an illusion. Self-definition is created through psychical boundaries at the same time that boundaries are created through self-definition. Both are experiential in nature and both originate through the disentangling of subjectivity and the objectification of experience.

In presentient intimate engagements, as in the deepest symmetrical mode of being, people *are* the other as well as themselves, and the other *is* them. Within the related unconscious, each person is his/her partner as each shares the other's subjectivity. Individuals then exist in dimensions governed by symmetrical being and subject relations. In a domain where asymmetry is more dominant, where object-relations theories are applicable, and where affiliative intimacy evolves, individuals *become* complements to one another. Each person allows the other to experience his/her self in a *becoming* fashion through a projective-introjective process in which dissociated psychic elements experienced as *unbecoming* by one individual are absorbed and encapsulated by the other. In either mode, people are constructed by the subjectivity of their partner, and they construct their partner's subjectivity.

Shared Subjectivity and "Doubling"

A number of psychoanalytic authors writing on twins, twinship, and "doubles" (such as shadows, reflections, imaginary companions, [Rank, 1925/1971; Bion, 1967; Abse, 1976; Arlow, 1960; Ortmeyer, 1970; Rucker, 1981]), have discussed the frequency, and perhaps universality, of phenomena related to the sharing of subjectivities. Double images, as well as symbols of opposites, have been understood to represent an unconscious pairing of bad and good that provides maximal psychic strength when this pairing creates a cohesive unit. Twins, in particular, can provide an accessible repository for each other for undesirable feelings. The twinship state maintains an unconscious phantasy that these traits are at each other's command, a state Ortmeyer calls the "we-self." The reciprocity of double relationships allows for the preservation and viability of needed psychic characteristics. The loss of the double partner often lessens the capacity for psychic functioning.

Participants in "double" phenomena seem to partake of a mutual subjectivity similar to that shared by intimate partners, and do so for similar purposes. However, the shared subjectivity inherent in the related unconscious is not primarily an artifact of an intimate relationship. Rather, the unconscious relationship is an artifact of the inherent dedifferentiation at the deepest level of symmetrical relations, and of the need to construct a shared subjectivity at a more asymmetrical level. The deep mutual resonance with each other's unconscious selves that coalesces into shared subjective experience is intuitively knowable because it is rooted in unity and indivisiveness. The qualities of a given intimate bond are extracted from this symmetrical base.

Racker's (1968) two forms of unconscious identifications, concordant and complementary, provide a working framework for our construction of intimacy. Racker described these two patterns of identification as distinguishable from one another, but not totally separated. Thus, they belong to the asymmetrical domain, but carry symmetrical properties. Concordant identifications, which form the basis for empathy and understanding, refer more to an unconscious recognition of psychic similarity between self and other, whereas complementary identifications comprise the rejection and projection of internal objects that foster difference. Using a subject-relations model, concordance is more aligned with the subjective mode of identification, whereas complementarity parallels the objective identificatory mode.

In a concordant identificatory process, one person senses in the other parts of the psyche similar to his/her own, allowing for the reception of these elements by the other. Unconsciously, the other recognizes these projections as familiar or acceptable and makes room for them as part of his or her self. In the contrasting complementary identificatory process, the person finds in another a refuge for the inner representations that are not integrated within his or her individual psychic self as it exists. The presentient aspects of intimacy rest more upon concordance, whereas the affiliative aspects of intimacy rest more upon complementarity. The presentient mode of intimacy is therefore more symmetrical in nature and thus is more inherently unconscious in form. The affiliative mode of intimacy has more asymmetrical and conscious characteristics and does not convey the same quality of intuitive knowing that characterizes presentient contacts.

In concordance, one party becomes the subject of the other's interior states, rather than the object of his or her projections. The self is subjectively experienced by the other through a psychic transformation from object to subject. This process is paralleled in subjective identification by the experience of the other through the experience of the self. The more conscious, getting-to-know-you aspects of relating and the building of shared experience serve as modes through which these unconscious concordant and subjective identifications can be expressed and made known within the relationship, but, in related unconscious dimensions, they do not create shared experience. In the related unconscious, shared experience encompasses the delineation and awareness of self and other.

In complementarity, it is the rejection and projection of internalized object representations that form the unconscious relational bond. One party becomes the object of the other's projections, creating a relationship based upon difference. Similarly, in objective identification, self is defined by the experience of other-than-self; experiences of other-than-self delineate individual boundaries. In either case, the relational process between the individuals, not only the individuals themselves, is necessary for the containment, evolution, and articulation of the original identifications that brought the two individuals together.

Sociobiological Reflections on Unconscious Relatedness

When viewed in this manner, not only are individuals on the lookout for an intimate partner, but they are led to do so by deeply unconscious psychic processes. Wright's (1994) ideas on unconscious experience in psychological evolution—in particular his thoughts on dating, romance, and marriage—have particular import for our discussion of intimacy. Wright posited that the unconscious mind was well developed and highly suited to the environment in which human beings existed prior to civilization and culture. Since evolutionary change requires millions of years to take form, humans remain psychobiologically adapted to a very different environment than civilization has wrought. Their deepest motives have remained linked to the primordial aim of transfering genes that is common to all biological life, rather than the morals, ideals, romantic longings, and contemporary behaviors that we prefer to think of as distinctly human. Contemporary abstractions and practices, according to Wright, including those regarding intimate pairing, have been culturally superimposed upon an archaic substratum designed within our ancestral environment for the purpose of carrying genetic material from one generation to another.

Wright cogently argued that, even after the arrival of language and self-awareness (or the evolution of asymmetrical logic in Matte-Blanco's terms), the press for genetic transmission, not species or individual selection, continues to dictate human behavior. Cultural emphases on either individual survival or the betterment of humankind as a group fly in the face of biology; the biological press for genetic transfer remains the underlying force in all biological life. Natural selection has had no reason to select against this primordial purpose and some reasons to sustain this function. Despite the evolutionary processes that have cultivated consciousness (or asymmetry), the primordial stratum in humans finds psychic expression in the unconscious (or symmetrical) mind. Even from a social Darwinian view, the motivational sources of human behavior have a deeper genesis and a more tele-scoped purpose than generally is ascertained.

Thus, mental life is thought from both sociobiological and psychoanalytic frames of reference to be directed by a basic, inclu-sive, unconscious process, despite the presence of consciousness awareness or asymmetrical functions. Both our understanding and Wright's contain the idea that unconscious process leads peo-ple to experiences toward which their conscious minds may not direct them, and that the substrate for interpersonal and emo-tional experience is broader and more inclusive than that which defines the experienced self. According to Wright, the vicissitudes of human courtship are designed to serve the preeminent uncon-scious evolutionary agenda of transferring genetic material, de-spite the loftier pretensions of romantic love and emotional attachment. In psychoanalytic thought, an analogy is found in the idea that unconscious relatedness is designed to aid the integra-tion of the basic psychical antipodes of unity and disunity, identi-fication and disidentification, despite other meanings that might be attributed consciously to a relationship.

Processes and Modes of Identification

In the service of such an agenda, our unconscious minds may lead us to find partners of one sort or another that develop into lasting, enriching relationships, or may lead us to engagements that do not move beyond certain parameters. Whether or not the two individuals sustain a relationship is not the critical variable in intimacy; in either case, aspects of one's unconscious may find a partner. In this process, the unconscious relationship between two people supersedes the bounds of their interpersonal relatedness.

The psychical knot is tied between affiliative partners by their need to remain connected with dissociated representations. Personality differences may exist in the interpersonal domain between presentient partners, but the resonance and synchrony in the unconscious realm of experience define their intimacy.

In Racker's thinking, love, empathy, and understanding are psychically based on a concordant pattern of identification. In the framework of Matte-Blanco's ideas, aggression and its deriviatives are inherently disunifying; thus, profound symmetry is more in conformity with love than with hate. Presentient intimacy and concordant identifications are reminiscent of the nature of deep symmetry, whereas affiliative intimacy and complementary identifications rely on more asymmetrical functioning. From a subject-relational premise, presentient intimacy and concordant identifications both rest upon the subjective identificatory modes that dominate in the symmetrical related unconscious. In comparison, affiliative intimacy and complementarity correspond to the objective identificatory modes that reflect more asymmetrical dimensions of experience.

What is unconsciously known in the experience of presentient intimacy is the sameness of two persons' unconscious realms and subjective experiences. Feelings of close, intense identification, the sense of being soul mates, the experience of passionate merger all flavor presentient bonds. Intimacy as shared psychical experience and as a source of creative discovery and expansion of consciousness (e.g., Wilner, 1975) within and between the individuals is more inherent in the presentient, than in the affiliative, mode. However, in its extreme, presentient intimacy may link two people in a deep emotional involvement in which differences are not well tolerated. Relationships skewed toward presentient intimacy in the extreme leave little room for individual growth. Ultimately, participants in such relationships may become incompatible as intimate partners because their mode of relatedness cannot withstand conflict or individuation.

Long-term, seemingly stable relationships that are felt by both participants as empty and unfulfilling represent the other prototypical extreme, that of intimacy rooted in complementary identifications. In affiliative experience, there may be a conscious understanding of the other person, mutual affection, a recognition of commonly shared experience, but there is not a deep, pervading sense of psychological fit or match and there is a tendency toward the depletion of vitality and creativity. Extreme affiliative connections foster alienation and disaffection that can render such relationships ultimately unsupportable.

Presentient and affiliative modes of intimacy, in their extremity, reflect diametrically opposed balances between asymmetry and symmetry. Affiliative relatedness is weighted towards differentiation via dissociation and toward the separatedness of subjective and objective experience. Thus, it is linked more directly to asymmetrical functions. Presentient relatedness is weighted toward dedifferentiation and unity and, thus, carries predominantly symmetrical properties. Although both presentient and affiliative modes of intimacy serve to integrate certain unconscious representations, the different equilibria that they present generate a felt experience and an emotional tilt that are qualitatively different.

In relationships based principally upon objective identifications, two people may share common experiences and life structures—perhaps for many years—but they do not experience an intuitive sense of knowing the other person from the inside out. They do not experience each other from a primarily symmetrical mode of being. A dominance of complementarity can hold a relationship together in a socially proscribed form, creating a superficially balanced relationship, but the element of concordant resonance is truncated or missing. Working to build intimacy can lead to a superficial understanding of each other's feelings and dynamics, but a concordant experience is not available unless the unconscious identifications shift away from projection, objectification, and difference and toward introjection, subjectification, and similarity.

Affiliative relatedness often embodies the feeling that, despite years of time together, the two persons have little in common. When examined closely, this experience is true on multiple levels. The feeling of having little in common is "in" affiliative relatedness in a very basic way. In affiliative relatedness, many intimate partners do have little in common, except for their common (shared) experience of little. This customary used descriptive phrase of little-in-common exemplifies the multidimensionality of identificatory positions in intimate relatedness and, as such, is worthy of detailed attention.

In affiliative connections, based largely upon complementary and objectifive identifications, aspects of the subject's self that were dissociated coalesce as psychical representations *in opposition to* the experienced self. Since the unlike representations that are exchanged by affiliative partners engender the experience of the other as different from the self, in predominantly affiliative experience, partners have little in common in the simplest sense of that phrase; they share very little common ground. (This shall be referred to as Meaning 1.)

Although superficially some relationships may appear to be fully affiliative, a mix of both presentient and affiliative qualities are present in all relationships. Both presentient and affiliative qualities can form around a core of subjective-concordant identifications that can exist within a objective-complementary identificatory matrix. Little-in-common can then be understood as the subjective-concordant core of an otherwise objective-complementary identificatory process. Under these conditions, an affiliative engagement with another has its unconscious roots in dissociated experiences of deprivation and isolation that are concordant between the two people, leaving the rest of the relationship to develop around difference and asynchrony, the consequence of projected inner representations. What the two individuals then share is the common experience of little (deprivation); having little is what they have in common. (This shall be referred to as Meaning 2.)

One of the ways in which the experience of little-in-common can be explicated is through the unconscious recognition of the mutual experience of deprivation that remains dissociated. To the extent that the deprivation is not symbolized or consciously accessible, it remains dissociated. The differences between the intimate companions are made overt, while the shared experience of deprivation (of little) remains deeply unconscious and may take such concrete forms as making oneself little, belittling, feeling little in the relationship, and having little to share.

Presentient and affiliative modes of intimacy are distinguished by the relative preponderance of subjective vs. objective identificatory modes of relating that are present. In affiliative intimacy, an extensive overlay of complementary identifications within the objective identificatory mode foreclose subjective-concordant experience, leaving the experience of little-in-common as the sole concordant connection. In presentient intimacy, pockets of complementarity may exist, but only within an overarching concordant identificatory matrix. Any complementary identifications are overshadowed by the dominant concordant representations and the corresponding subjective identificatory mode.

Affiliative intimacy, in harboring mostly complementary identifications, engenders a togetherness distinguished by difference and alienation, and framed by properties of asymmetry. The togetherness in this togetherness-of-difference is the bridge to the deeply underlying symmetrical unity of the intimate partners. This unity is otherwise obscured by the asymmetrical properties of a bond that highlights differences. Presentient intimacy, rooted in subjective-concordant identification, engenders a togetherness characterized by similarity and familiarity, which is more fully linked to the symmetrical unconscious.

The concordant-within-complementary conceptualization incorporates the deep and surface meanings of experiences such as little-in-common, which the complementary-only conceptualization does not. Little-in-common conveys a literal or surface communication that is readily apprehended as well as a deeper communication that can only be understood in a layered metaphorical sense. The symbolic meaning of little-in-common requires a convolution of the more facile mode of understanding. This convolution shows the complexity of the seemingly simple turn of phrase. The dual nature of this communication captures the concordant-within-complementary pattern; commonality is embedded in dissimilarity, just as Meaning 2 of little-in-common is embedded linguistically in Meaning 1. The layering of meanings, in this illustration, exemplifies the potential for the multidimensionality of experience and contexts that denote related unconscious process.

This multidimensionality makes the concordance-within-complementary model a richer explanation of presentient and affiliative intimacy than does a model that sees these two forms of intimacy as dichotomous and mutually exclusive. The dialectics it implies are in keeping with the schema of symmetry and asymmetry as interpenetrating and perpetually fluctuating. Intimate relationships are not only affiliative or presentient, but contain a mixture of objective-complementary and subjective-concordant aspects. This idea is consistent with Racker's observation that concordance and complementarity can be differentiated, but are not fully separable. The creation of a full intimacy, whether in a marriage, a friendship, or an analysis, requires concordant and complementary identifications, objective and subjective identificatory experiences, and the symmetrical and asymmetrical properties that the relationship comprises. The challenge for intimate partners engaging in predominantly presentient relatedness is the incorporation of complementary identifications, objective identificatory modes, and asymmetrical experience into their relationship. The challenge posed to intimate partners engaging in predominantly affiliative relatedness is to create room for subjective, concordant, symmetrical, experience. In all viable intimate dyads, there are dialectical vacillations between objectification and subjectification, concordance and complementarity, symmetry and asymmetry, presentience and affiliation.

The process of making transformations between modes and types of identification, akin to the shifting of figure-ground experience, is fostered through the unfolding of symmetrical experience, not through improved communication skills or conscious inquiry per se. In the fullness of either state of intimate relatedness, the participants in the relationships come to experience themselves from the place of the other, as well as from the place of the self, and to experience the other from within themselves. What they see in the other is in them, and what is in them comes to be seen in the other. The transformative process, which links modes of experience that have been disconnected, promotes psychic integration and the feeling of psychic wholeness, as well as cultivating a sense of wholeness and integration in one's relatedness with others.

Each individual in intimate connection with another is, thus, both the figure and the ground in relation to the other. Each sometimes represents those dissociated identifications that constitute the figure, sometimes represents those that define the ground, and at other times holds both elements in equilibrium simultaneously. The relationship between two individuals is the context in which the figure-ground shifts. Each individual also can be alternately either the figure or the ground vis a vis the other and vis a vis the relationship.

INTIMACY AND LOSS OF INTIMACY AS LIVED EXPERIENCES

The recognition that our intimate relationships are shaped by the figure and the ground of our known and unknown selves and the known and unknown selves of the other, rather than by interactions between wholly consolidated individuals, positions us to experience relational shifts from a creative vantage point. Our intimate experiences are no longer confined by the understandings that we are doing something, that something is being done to us, or even that we are doing something together to each other. Rather, it begins to reveal the possibility that we are doing something *through* each other and that something is being done *through* us. Metaphorically, we are not only the subject or the object, or subject-object configuration, but the person both feeling and creating the experience. We become intimate subjects.

Something living through us, psychologically and physiologically, has been described by Groddeck (1923/1949). Groddeck's concept of the "It" (upon which which Freud's concept of "id" was founded) depicts just such a process. The It refers to the life force in each of us, which can be found in every cell, organ, and organ system in our bodies, as well as in the realm of the psyche. Like Matte-Blanco's symmetry, It is larger, and more inclusive than our conscious minds and has its own agenda unbeknownst to us. Only with much introspection, can we partially become aware of the mechanisms and the agenda of It. In this introspective process, unconscious aspects of our psyche and soma find new equilibrium, and lead us to more integrated states of being. In becoming intimate subjects, we come closer to these facets of psychic experience as they are manifest in the relational realm.

The coming together of dissociated psychic entities and of two unconscious selves brings with it the inevitability of separation. The closeness inherent in any intimate connection, even a transitory one, carries with it the potential experience of loss. Loss of the other, in either presentient or affiliative intimacy and in regard to either concordant or complementary identifications, entails a correspondent loss of part of the self. As unconscious identifications are assimilated by another and through the relationship with that other, the self as it is then known is lost. Through this change, the earlier nature of the experienced self is extinguished by the very unconscious relational process that had enlivened its unknown side.

The literal loss of an intimate partner constitutes not only the loss of that individual and its tangible repercussions, but also the loss of the relational process that encompasses the intimacy. The experience of mourning for an intimate partner involves a recognition of the loss of the person as other, the person as part the self, the self as part of the other person, and the unconscious relatedness that bind these together. While identificatory processes can lead one person to internalize aspects of another, processes of unconscious relatedness are more dependent on mutual experience and less readily internalized. Loss often leaves in its wake[1] a phantom experience, the sense that something that is missing is still felt. What is felt is the subjective experience of the other in relation to the self. What is missing is the related unconscious context in which subject and object are transformed, symmetrical/asymmetrical unfolding evolves, and mutual subjectivities are exchanged. The individual psychic realm remains, forever imprinted by the relationship with the lost individual, but the related unconscious realm that defined and was defined by their relatedness no longer exists.

---

[1] In the mourning after a wake, the morning after a wake, or in the morning after one awakens, the loss of the external or internal other is re-experienced in the loss and regaining of the conscious self. In loss, part of the self is experienced as irrecovably missing and simultaneously the self is redefined as entire. The various combinations and permutations of morning and mourning, and wake as death, wake as life, and wake as trailing behind, represent a collapse of discriminated meanings that exemplifies a symmetrization of meaning.

PRESENTIENCE AND AFFILIATION
IN THE ANALYTIC DYAD

Ironically, the psychoanalytic relationship, whose expressed purpose is to foster psychic growth and evolution, is too often an arena for the truncation of intimacy and the foreclosure of mutually subjective experience. The traditional psychoanalytic relationship founded upon anonymity and neutrality does not foster the fullest possible appreciation of the subjectivity of patient and analyst. The conventional psychoanalytic model is predicated upon processes of objectification and projection, whereby the patient projects onto the analyst and experiences the analyst as other. Occasionally, and under much less desirable circumstances, the analyst projects upon the patient. This theoretical model and its correlate clinical approach preclude intimacy because they preclude the transformation of object into subject. Projection alone does not permit subject-subject experience; rather, it keeps subject and object separate.

Within analytic intimacy, the patient (subject) must be experienced as *of* the self, not just *in* the self. While much of analytic relatedness is conducted in an asymmetrical dimension, there needs to be room in the analytic dyad for symmetrical experience. In the weakest form of symmetrical experience, the patient's representations (the other) are felt either as familiar or unfamiliar (concordant or complementary) to the analyst, but the patient's projections remain recognizable as such. In the intensity of deeper dimensions of symmetrical experience, the patient's projective contributions are felt as indistinguishable from the self of the analyst, and the relational process by which subject and object are made distinct is not recognizable. Only then is the patient truly— and intimately—known.

Most contemporary psychoanalysts no longer hold to a strictly classical approach of objectivity and distance, but to the extent that they do, such intimacy is relegated to an arena outside the consulting room. Whether a given psychoanalytic connection originates in concordant or complementary identifications, subjective or objective identificatory modes, or is poised for presentient or affiliative intimacy, an analytic posture that works to sustain objectivity is destined to keep subject and object distinct.

This traps the analytic relationship within the asymmetrical mode and inevitably compromises intimacy.

The intimate knowing of the patient on the part of the analyst requires an openness to the intimate knowing of the analyst on the part of the patient. This experience of knowing need not be one of conscious self-disclosure, but one of related unconscious experience of the patient-in-the-analyst and the analyst-in-the-patient. At intimate junctures in an analysis, the patient may be felt as the analyst to the analyst, and the analyst may be felt as patient to the patient. Many analytic dyads are never open to this experience, because it challenges illusions of psychic separateness and threatens to expose narcissistic vulnerabilities. Patient-analyst intimacy, along with all the psychic material that it might contain, then remains unpotentiated and becomes dissociated from the analytic space. One reflection of this dissociation can be glimpsed in the paradox that one is free to discuss intimate subjects in analysis, whereas the subject of intimacy in analysis is less freely discussed.

When perceived through asymmetrical understanding, intimacy forms a basic modality through which human beings assuage a sense of isolation and incompleteness. In this perspective, it comprises both an unconscious relational experience and, secondarily, a consciously experienced interpersonal alliance. It can allow an individual to experience a basic sense of connection without necessitating the full sacrifice of personal identity. When viewed from a more symmetrical space, intimacy reflects our inherent communal unity; isolation and incompleteness reflect the translation of symmetrical experience into asymmetrical modes of being. From this position, an unconscious intimate tie can emerge without interpersonal sequelae. Given only a surface glance, two individuals in intimate connection can never really be inside the experience of each other. Upon a closer look, however, our intimate relationships as consciously experienced may be only the shadow of the connections between people. When seen this way, people are not only drawn together from positions of separateness, but also are pulled apart by strivings for consciousness and psychic distinction. Intimacy is one link to the primal experiences of psychic unity and disunity.

10

WORDS TO THE WISE ON THE WISDOM IN SUBJECT RELATIONS

Naomi Rucker

The scientific and technological advances of the twentieth century have been equated in the minds of many with providing answers for the fundamental questions of the human condition. Adler (1992), in his lexicon of essays synopsizing the definitive ideas and discourse of Western thought over the last twenty-five hundred years, called this state of affairs the "twentieth-century

Note: Portions of this chapter were excerpted from Rucker, 1994, "Exploratory Thoughts on Wisdom, Intimacy, and Analytic Relatedness," *American Journal of Psychoanalysis*, 54(2).

delusion," a grandiose delusion that flagrantly disregards the wisdom of previous epochs (p. ix). The scientific and technological advances, which constitute a body of knowledge that is deemed unequivocally superior in this distorted vision of our times, emanated from the positivistic tradition, itself grounded in objectivity, that has dominated intellectual endeavor in this century. As we approach the millennium, positivism is showing signs of descendency. There is now room in intellectual debate to argue for the value and meaning of subjectivity. Within psychoanalysis, subjectivity has begun its ascendancy.

In this intellectual atmosphere, we can begin to integrate (or reintegrate) into our concept of psychic life, constructs such as wisdom, which had gone by the wayside during the supremacy of positivism. I recently addressed the interface between wisdom and analytic process by asserting that wisdom evolves within a relational context and that psychoanalysis is in a choice position to bring that process to fruition (Rucker, 1994). We expand the notion that relatedness is central to the emergence of wisdom by emphasizing the importance of subject relatedness to the cultivation of wisdom.

PREMISES OF WISDOM

Principles of wisdom can be traced to the philosophical and religious thought of ancient cultures, as expressed in the literature of the Old and New Testament, and in the books of pagan antiquity. Ancient Western philosophers developed ideas of wisdom originating in axioms of reason and the perfection of intellect, whereas religious perspectives on wisdom tended to infuse wisdom with issues of moral character (Adler, 1992). In contrast to the development of Western thought, which contains this dichotomy between philosophical and religious perspectives, societies of the ancient East considered wisdom to relate to man's attunement with the inner self and with universal natural law, and to the development of higher levels of consciousness and enlightenment (Dittman-Kohli and Baltes, 1990). Wise individuals in many cultures, past and present, are or have been highly valued and esteemed for their age and experience. The veneration of elders and the veneration of wisdom have gone hand-in-hand with social stability and tradition.

Early Western philosophers viewed wisdom as uniting knowledge and action by incorporating the dialectic between good and evil into the attainment of wisdom, emphasizing the quality of one's judgment about the external world. Wisdom, the supreme virtue of (hu)mankind, was felt to exist as much in the realm of conduct as that of thought. Its special character lay in its dual concerns with the ultimate nature of things and with the ultimate good for (hu)mankind. Fundamental to a wise mind was thought to be a state of inner peace, repose, and harmony between reason and one's soul. For Plato, it was the soul that gave rise to knowledge, and, as the faculty of knowledge, the soul that both directs conduct and contemplates truth (Adler, 1992).

These early ideas about wisdom were infused with a richness that contemporary perspectives no longer embrace. In Adler's opinion, the ancients held wisdom in greater esteem and cultivated a greater understanding of it than most modern societies. Over the centuries, wisdom was distinguished by ideas about humankind that were not found in art, science, or any other form of knowledge or learning. As time has passed, theology and philosophy have been superseded by the scientific method, and wisdom has come to be associated largely with ancient thought. Consequently, the contemporary relevance of wisdom has been lost; modern ideas find their acceptability in science. As Adler states, knowledge can be steadily increased and learning can advance, but wisdom does not progress accordingly. Scientific/technological advancement has not brought wisdom. In Adler's words, "The individual may grow in wisdom. The race does not seem to" (p. 938).

Contemporary thinking tends to examine wisdom from within the domain of cognition and intelligence, but to separate it from objective problem solving. There is little agreement on the defining characteristics of wisdom, but a general consensus exists that wisdom has little or no value in the realm of the objective—that is the domain of science. Definitions of wisdom lack consistency and breadth, and often are complex and obscure, but they seldom include a role for nonintellectual abilities or gifts.

(Dittman-Kohli and Baltes, 1990). In modern psychological thought, much more attention to wisdom has been paid by the fields of cognitive psychology and life span developmental psychology than by psychoanalysis. The particular meaning and importance of wisdom to the ontological, existential realm that psychoanalysis occupies has been neglected.

Clayton (1982) presents a model of wisdom that has some psychoanalytic relevance, although her vantage point is not psychoanalytic. She differentiates wisdom from intelligence by incorporating the consideration of the consequences of one's actions to self and others to wisdom. Wisdom, in her view, is essentially the ability to understand human nature. Evolving over the course of a lifetime, wisdom forms a basis for the development of intelligence. Intelligence, in contrast to wisdom, is a less ambiguous construct that concerns logical thought, abstract conceptualization, and the accomplishment of life-sustaining tasks. Clayton tentatively poses an alliance between relations among people and the presence of the capacity to be wise that we endorse and find highly relevant to relational theory.

THE RELATIONAL CONTEXT FOR WISDOM

From a relational perspective, wisdom is constructed through interpersonal relations and, specifically, stems from mutual subjective experience. Insight into human nature, such as Clayton denotes, has a particular connection with subjectivity. In its fullest expression, wisdom embodies capacities for compassion, empathy, and the ability to appreciate another's perspective from both intellectual and emotional domains. Yet, even in more limited expression, wisdom requires the capacity to organize experience using multiple frames of reference. To be wise, one must rely upon both object-oriented mentation and subject-oriented experience. Wisdom requires the ability to augment asymmetrical thought with access to the multilayered symmetrical substrate from which such thought emanates. The present cultural bias towards intellect and intellectualization and its corresponding emphasis on asymmetrical, objective thought have compromised the apprehension of multidimensional experience. As Oliner (1988) points out, a hyperinvestment in intellect leads to the suppression of other kinds of knowledge.

The shift in Western culture from stable, traditional societies to those marked by rapid change, paralleled the substitution of esteem for the wise by esteem for the smart. Knowledge and intelligence have come to mean the swift acquisition of information, while other kinds of enlightenment, such as intuition or relational and emotional awareness, are devalued. The collapse of concepts of wisdom into the domain of cognitive psychology reflects the suppression of subjectivity and mimics an underlying cultural confusion between knowledge and sagacity.

While intellect transmits information, wisdom captures the experiential and the subjective in a culture. As Plato recognized, wisdom embodies a sense of soul. Bettelheim (1982) writes of the loss of soul in psychoanalysis in the translation of Freud's work from its original German to a scientific style of English from which American psychoanalysis originated. By courting acceptance of the scientific community, American psychoanalysis promoted theoretical models that strive for objectivity and approximations of scientific precision. These models have focused psychoanalytic thought in directions counter to the appreciation of the wisdom in subjectivity. The recent shifts in the orientation of psychoanalysis toward the realm of the subjective have occasioned a recognition that subjectivity is a wellspring for wisdom.

What makes one wise is not solely or even largely experiences with problems or tasks—even interpersonal tasks—but rather, deep, multilayered connections with others. Through relationships, our intellect, emotion, and subjective experience are integrated. In understanding human relationships to be only intra-psychically or object driven, we deny ourselves the wisdom that comes with knowing another from the inside out, confining ourselves to limited layers of meaning and meaningfulness. In making this concession to objectivity and self-definition, we blind ourselves to the kind of wisdom found only through subject relations.

Relational wisdom is not always expressed in ordinary ways. It is not always directed through processes of intellect or cognitively mediated to the same extent as knowledge. Often it is seen in metaphor, dream imagery, and double entendre, as well as in subtle turns of phrase and slips of the tongue that can exhibit brilliance and presence of mind. The difference between metaphor and simile exemplifies the difference between more relational and more intellectual wisdoms and identifies their respective symmetric and asymmetric underpinnings. A more direct link to unconscious symmetry occurs in symbolic metaphor in which one entity is described as being another. In contrast, simile is anchored in asymmetrical parallel by which properties or things are equated by their resemblance. Being another implies the mutual identity that points to symmetrical experience. Resemblance implies the discreteness that hallmarks asymmetrical functions.

Relational wisdom is commonly an intuitive knowledge, intuitive in the sense of Langer (1966), natural, spontaneous, not entailing deliberate thought or action. Such wisdom often springs from the immediate dynamics of an interpersonal relationship or situation, rather than as a communication of knowledge about the external world. Because it is not objective, this kind of wisdom is not usually recognized as such. Yet, what appears superficially to be simplistic and insignificant in its lack of intellectual, objective content is often very wise and insightful in its meaning and depth. The following examples highlight multidimensionality and process and avoid obscuring these elements with content. At first, these illustrations may not seem noteworthy, but it is in their multidimensionality that one finds their worth, and in their naive simplicity that their complexity and wisdom are revealed.

Sarah

A very successful businesswoman who had sold her business in order to stay home and care for her young children related the following incident to her analyst: Her very young daughter said to her while getting dressed in the morning, "I'm Sarah and I'm a girl, and he's Danny and he's a boy, and you're [just] a mother." The patient was particularly struck by her daughter's definitive tone that captured the constriction of identity that this mother had been feeling privately since staying at home with her children.

She no longer felt fully like an adult woman with an individual identity, only like a mother defined by her children and her role with them. Sarah's statement imparted a sense of wisdom about how her mother felt within herself. The surface meaning of Sarah's remark was built upon complementary identifications and objective identificatory modes that stress difference, yet the emergence of this comment was concordant and subjective in nature. Clearly, Sarah and her mother were different individuals in different positions in life, but they were also the same. Sarah recognized her mother's position because they shared the same related unconscious experience of the mother as only a mother. This shared subject relationship made it necessary for Sarah to define her own personhood in order to delineate her difference from her mother.

Anne

A young woman, Anne, was visited by her father briefly and unexpectedly. He walked into and out of her home in only a few moments, and said very little, even though he had not seen her for many weeks. When he left she commented to a friend with humor, "My father came to tell me that he loved me . . . in my family you have to be paranoid to figure these things out." Later she said, "He'll never understand me, but it doesn't matter any more because I understand him." To those around her, the observation that he visited to express his love seemed ludicrous, given the brevity and apparent purposelessness of his stay, but she was somehow able to fit herself inside his experience to receive his very covert communication.

Many years later, after much reflection on this incident, Anne's friend understood that she was right, that her father did visit to show his love. It was only in the mutual subjective connection between this father and daughter that this tacit communication was fathomable. Her comment about understanding her father was a wise one. It conveyed their deep connection with each other, but it also expressed the use of that connection to comprehend something very valuable about the evolution of relationships. It reflected both object and subject dimensions of being. In this example the meaning of the flow between symmetry and asymmetry, concordance and complementarity, and object and subject relatedness that gives rise to wisdom is apparent. The surface quality of the interaction between this daughter and her father conveyed detachment and complementarity, while its deeper quality conveyed concordance and connection.

Anne's need to be paranoid reflected the overriding asymmetrical coding of their connection. Only from an asymmetrical vantage point, one of differentiation and separation, was paranoia necessary for her to understand her father's motives. Anne had to be paranoid about her father only to the extent that she moved away from their mutual subjectivity into more individuated objectified experience. Paranoia allows one to keep a foothold in the realm of asymmetry when symmetrical experience is dominant. From an asymmetrical position, the subject (or self) must invade the boundaries of the object (or other), or be invaded by him to know him. From a symmetrical position, the self already experiences the other subjectively because there are no boundaries through which he is objectified. Hence from a subject-relational position, there are no grounds for paranoia.

Anne, in occupying a relational space with her father, unconsciously resonated with him, despite appearances to the contrary. As Anne recognized, he may never have come to understand her in an objective sense, as a fully articulated individual, but she could experience his connectedness to her. Although their object-related appreciation of one another may well have been unbalanced, leaving Anne with the onus of objective understanding, their subjective relatedness was not in question. Objectively, she could only make sense of his behavior by hyperattentiveness (paranoia), but subjectively his intent was clear to her.

Dr. Ross

A different (and of course similar) example is found in a family therapy situation with a schizophrenic patient and his family and a seasoned, well-respected analyst. During one session, the mother was hostile and seemingly cruel to her schizophrenic son to a degree that was quite upsetting to the hospital staff. Dr. Ross made the very sapient comment to the staff that the mother-son interaction is the way they show love for one another. Whether one agrees that this is an expression of love or something else, this example shows the fundamental way in which this mother and son connected.

Here, again, we see the surface structure of a relational exchange reflecting complementarity and objectivity, while the deep structure of their relatedness holds concordance and mutual subjectivity. What appeared to others to be hostility, rage, and the enactment of complementary identification also carried the relational meaning of contact and concordance to them. What was objectified as hostility and sadism was subjectively coded as attachment. The perennial and pervasive subject-relatedness with a concomitant lack of object-relatedness, that is reflected in their interactions, and a corresponding dominance of symmetry over asymmetry, rendered this kind of interchange psychotic. In contrast to the symmetrical entrenchment of this psychotic communication, Dr. Ross' remarks address the dialectic between inner and outer experience and perception with intuition and ease; his ability to do so is what makes his simple statement wise.

THE SUBJECTIVE RELATIONAL MATRIX

Wisdom is born in a flow and flexibility between symmetrical and asymmetrical modes of being. In the examples given, Anne and Sarah gave voice to their unconscious experience of mutual subjectivity and its symmetrical and asymmetrical properties, whereas Dr. Ross served the function of translating between symmetrical and asymmetrical dimensions. This interplay between modes of being and the facilitation of the integration of experiential dimensions comprise the fundaments for wisdom. These characteristics cannot be found apart from the subjective-relational matrix.

Anne and Sarah portray different points of balance in the shifts between subjectivity-objectivity and symmetry-asymmetry. Sarah's wisdom captured themes customarily associated with childhood, but reflected the dialectical interrelationship of these themes that is often overlooked. The movement toward separatedness and distinction of self, that is often considered preeminent in childhood, is paralleled in Sarah's remarks by the simultaneous experience of sameness and unity. Intuitive affective communications and connection between Sarah and her mother existed unconsciously, while difference and differentiation were articulated consciously. Here, the objective/projective-subjective/introjective exchanges between mother and child regarding self-definition are discernable in relatively undisguised form, as opposed to the more derivative forms in which they are observable in adult life.

Anne depicts a wisdom often more characteristic of adult life, in which problematic identifications have been rendered less problematic, allowing for both self-distinction and empathy with another to be held in conscious experience. Anne, who had a developed sense of differentiation and psychic separateness, needed to move toward an appreciation of her symmetrical, subjective engagement with her father to understand the perplexing quality of their relationship, whereas Sarah's challenge appeared in the shift toward asymmetrical disengagement and self-definition. Sarah, being centered at that moment in the experience of sameness with her mother, sought to balance that sameness with an articulation of their differences. Anne spoke from a more differentiated position, needing to articulate the experience of connection and resonance for a sense of integration. Yet, in both these illustrations, the co-existence of subjectivity and objectivity are given expression.

Although these case examples may seem to support traditional developmental notions that autonomy of self moves along a chronological path in childhood, it is the differences in the relatedness between Sarah and her mother and Anne and her father that are essential, not age. While the move towards asymmetry and differentiation may have some developmental valence, shifts between symmetrical-asymmetrical and subjective-objective modes are present at all ages, as is the potential for wisdom that such flexibility permits. Psychological development and psychical experience are portrayed through Sarah and Anne as relational, fluid, nonlinear, and multilayered, in contrast to the unidirectional and hierarchal models of development exemplified by conventional ideas such as developmental lines and phases, and in the common association of wisdom with chronological maturity.

Anne and Sarah were able to make the translation between symmetrical and asymmetrical engagement themselves within their respective relational contexts, whereas Dr. Ross' clinical family was not. In making his comment, Dr. Ross served an interpersonal linking function between the subject-oriented world of the patients and the object-oriented one of the staff that corresponded to the translation between symmetrical and asymmetrical engagement. He gave voice to the related unconscious between mother and son, bridging poles of difference and similarity, symmetry and asymmetry, subjectivity and objectivity, consciousness and unconsciousness. He enabled idiosyncratic communication to have consensual meaning, transforming interior, private experience of self into shared and communicable self-other experience.

In this mother-son pair, the interior private nature of experience was shared between them, but was peculiar to their dyad and incomprehensible to others. Their relational system formed a kind of dyadic self, bounded by the idiosyncrasies and incomprehensibility of their relatedness; others may have been delineated as "other", in significant measure, by their inability to comprehend this unconscious system. This example, in particular, illuminates wisdom as emanating from within the realm of unconscious relatedness, rather than within one or another individual. Interior experience was interior to this dyad, not only internal to each individual. The idiosyncratic nature of this mother-son connection formed a protective boundary for the integrity of the dyad in a similar fashion to the definition and integrity of self that individual boundaries provide. The difference in the capacities for translation seen in this family and in Anne or Sarah, in conjunction with the dyadic self it illustrates, are points of distinction between that which is designated as psychotic and that which is not.

Although asymmetrical coding may be required for wisdom to be communicated, access to symmetrical experience is necessary for wisdom to be present and for it to be heard. This access is made possible by a linking, translative, or transformative function. This function exists within the individual psyches of well-integrated persons (or persons at moments of integration), such as Anne and Sarah, or it can be provided by an individual who unconsciously serves as an auxiliary bridge in the interpersonal realm when internal translation is not possible. This latter instance was the case with Dr. Ross and his clinical family. In the absence of either internal or interpersonal translation, the dimensionality and fluidity that foster wisdom are markedly constrained and psychic experience remains unintegrated.

When the openness to symmetry is impeded, one can only hear the asymmetrical meanings of a communication, missing the many possible layers of meaning that make something wise. Seen only from an asymmetrical position, many things seem flat, simplistic, and unremarkable. Conversely, if one is immersed in symmetrical experience, communications can be multilayered and symbolic, but often too personalized and idiosyncratic to be construed as wise. In the extreme, such communications are defined as psychotic, which, in this context, sometimes may stand in opposition to wise.

Thus, the potential for wisdom resides in both the sender and the receiver (the subject and the object) and in the relational unconscious space that they occupy together. The thoughts and ideas that emerge from this amorphous space as wisdom are only fragments of that which is available in unpotentiated form. Although wisdom can be nourished by life experience and by the opportunities that living offers for engagement in a range of human relationships, its essence lies in the dyadic related unconscious and in the fluidity between modes of experience. It is through the synergism inherent in subject relations that the omnipresent potential for wisdom is transformed into something new, different, and distinguishable as wise. Through anaclitic translation, undifferentiated potential (and unpotentiated differentiation) develop parameters and becomes both definable and defined as wisdom.

Thus, the manifestation of wisdom requires two subjects who are also objects, and whose relationship is experienced concurrently in both subject and object dimensions. Bion has suggested that we are compelled to think because we meet thoughts that already exist (Bleandonu, 1994). In the right subject-subject relation, the thoughts that we meet can emerge in conscious-relatedness as wise.

11

THE POLITICAL AND THE PERSONAL
CULTURAL EXPRESSIONS OF IDENTIFICATION AND DISIDENTIFICATION

Karen Lombardi and Naomi Rucker

The identifications and disidentifications that frame the dialectic between self and other also scaffold the relationship between the individual and his/her cultural surround. Cultural distinctions, such as class, race, and gender, dichotomize human qualities, ignoring more subtle gradations in sameness or difference. Thus, we speak of opposite sexes, blacks and whites, rich and poor more readily than we conceptualize the variations and combinations within and between categories of gender, race, and class. This polarization is reinforced by judgements of superiority or inferiority.

The understanding of cultural distinctions and categorizations often rests upon assumptions regarding the primacy of nature vs. the primacy of nurture, biology/genetics vs. environment/society. Assumptions on both sides of the nature-nurture debate counter-pose a fundamental experience of biological self to an equally fundamental experience of an other than biological-self. Yet, these assumptions are founded upon more basic identificatory positions regarding the dialectics between subject-object, inner-outer, similarity and dissimilarity. The nature-nurture controversy exists as an undercurrent in contemporary discourse on culture and society, but is rarely depicted as metaphor for self-other experience. An understanding of the relationship between the political and the personal and of the roots of this relationship in the nature-nurture debate has been hampered by a lack of appreciation of dialectical relatedness in unconscious experience.

Arguments for the preeminence of biology/genetics vs. arguments for the preeminence of environmental/social forces in the genesis of psychological or cultural phenomena are commonly presented as antithetical to each other, or as interacting from antithetical positions. Interactionism, in giving credence to both biological and environmental arguments, concludes that development involves both nature and nurture, but it does so with a dissatisfying generality. Interactionism does not meet the challenge of simultaneously integrating biology and environment and keeping them separate satisfactorily. If genetics and environment interact, then how are they separate and separable? If they are not distinguishable, then how do they interact?

Similar questions can be posed from the self-other discourse. If we are all other, how is it that we are different either biologically or psychologically? We are "other" than what? If we are all self, how is the impact of our environments explainable? From a viewpoint in which self and other interact, these interactions can be delineated only if self and other can be said to exist in pure form at some point. If interacting elements are never pure, then what is it that interacts and what does that interaction mean?

A dialectical emphasis and an appreciation of multidimensional unconscious experience permit phenomena that appear static, self-contained, and mutually exclusive to be considered as

coexisting in states of embeddedness and states of distinction at
the same time. Phenomena then are seen as mutually constituted, synergistic and interpenetrating elements within a larger
dynamic whole. One crucible of the dialectical position, that an
individual element is always distinct from those elements with
which it is unified (Hegel, 1817/1965; Kosok, 1970) allows
disparate positions, such as biological vs. environmental primacy, to be framed in terms of shifts between unity and disunity, identification and disidentification. This principle moves
theory beyond static dichotomies and their intermediary, the
notion of interactionism.

THE BIOLOGY AS ENVIRONMENT
AND THE ENVIRONMENT AS BIOLOGY

Evolutionary psychology and sociohistorical constructivism
mark two poles of the nature-nurture discourse. They are roughly
paralleled in psychoanalysis by classical drive theory on one hand,
which is consistent with many Darwininan principles and promotes psychobiological motivation in psychic life, and self psychology and certain renditions of interpersonal theory on the
other hand, which underscore environmental influences on psychical experience. The psychoanalytic analog to an interactionist
position falls within the domain of object-relation theories. Evolutionary psychology, alongside classical drive theory, stands in
the familiar territory of biological determinism, while constructivism attempts to account for seemingly biologically-rooted phenomena through social processes. Wright (1994), who discusses
human psychology from the domain of contemporary Darwinism, and Vygotsky (1978), perhaps the original social constructivist, can be seen to represent, respectively, the nature and the
nurture positions.

Evolutionary psychology, to which the nature-nurture debate
is central, has put forth the notion that human behavior is geared
not toward the selection of the species or of the individual, but toward the transmission of genetic material alone. Wright (1994)
elaborates this theory with the premise that the ultimate mission

of the unconscious mind is to serve the primordial aim of transferring genes, an aim that is common to all biological life. The
unconscious serves this aim through engendering complex self-
deceptions that may place conscious thought at great variance
from this fundamental purpose. Thus, human morality, ideals, relationships, and so on are complicated disguises for the biological
thrust toward DNA transmission. Yet, both aspects of humanity
and the process of their disguise have a covert evolutionary logic,
designed to service this basic biological directive. Wright's view
subordinates unconscious process to evolutionary dictates and
constructs it as an artifact of biology. Wright is interested in explicating the "animal essence at the core of the unconscious"
(p. 314). From his vantage point, the roots of unconscious process would be found in the genetic material that lives on beyond
the lifetime of an individual or of a species.

Theorists whose ideas are consistent with a constructivist paradigm, such as Vygotsky (1978) and Langer (1966), handle the
antimony between biological and environmental determinism by
placing biology and psychology on different planes of abstraction
where they are interdependent, but nondetermining. Langer and
Vygotsky, along with Matte-Blanco, see unconscious process and
psychological phenomena as existing in their own right, neither
subordinate nor supraordinate to biology.

Langer (1966) views psychical matters as irreducible to their
physiological underpinnings, averring that meaning and symbolization constitute an order of experience apart from physiology. For
Vygotsky, mind is a social product founded upon a threshold of biological adequacy, but developing according to its own independent principles once this threshold has been reached. Human
evolution is dictated by culture; the cultural organization of biological elements creates mind. Matte-Blanco asserts that the deepest
unconscious dimensions exist without biological motivation; they
are present as primary unconscious experience, not derivative of biology or repression. Instinct, considered to be a source of psychological motivation emanating from biological processes, first
appears at an asymmetrical level because it involves discrete states of
need; it is not present at deeper layers of experience and interfaces
with mental activity only at an intermediate or superficial plane.

From a Vygotskian position, mature psychological potential is realized through social mediation, not biological directive. It is the relative *lack* of intrinsic biological determination of behavior, in comparison to the more dominant and pervasive biological press present in nonhuman species, that allows human beings to develop a human psychology. Human psychology features the minimization of biological directives; biology guides behavior in humans by its absence, not by its presence. In Vygotsky's thinking, culture transforms physiological structure, thereby molding both mind and human evolution. Interpersonal relatedness, far more than biology, renders humans beings human. "The biological infant only becomes a psychological subject through participating in social relations" (p. 149). The absence of strict biological control over behavior requires that other capacities that are especially human (i.e., language, consciousness) develop in order to replace biological directives. The primary biological dictate in human psychology is the latitude given for people to construct themselves.

Language, for example, which is often viewed as genetically determined and biologically programmed, is understood from a Vygotskian perspective as important and universal precisely because biological control over communication is minimal. Symbolization and abstract reasoning, which are considered to distinguish human cognition and communication from that of other animals, are inspired by the need to communicate in a social context. The motivation for language to become a universal and readily acquired function, thus, for Vygotskian thinkers, is social, not biological.

Here, we have a "nurture" argument for an aspect of human psychic life that is often and easily construed to conform to a "nature" theoretical position. However, the data that language is universally and readily acquired can be, and is, adopted by both positions to explicate either biological or environmental principles. When these principles are placed in opposition to one another, with one as subject and the other as object, they cannot both be true. When they are positioned in interaction, mutual contributions to the linguistic phenomena are acknowledged, but they retain their essential identity as either environment or biology.

This essential identity is misleading. From a dialectical stance, both environment and biology are inherent properties of each other, rather than separate entities. They are concurrently subject and object, with shifting relative positions within a larger realm of relatedness between self and other. This dialectical view presents the biological elements of language, including integrated aspects of sociality, and the social elements of language including integrated aspects of biology, such that biology is environment and environment is biology. Biology and environment do not interact; rather, they mutually constitute one another and are indistinguishable in pure form. They are dialectically and bimodally interrelated. The universality of language represents the integrated wholeness of this biological-social configuration, not the preeminence of biology, environment, or of their interaction. Biology and environment appear to be separate domains only insofar as they are perceived asymmetrically as bivalent structures.

DETERMINISM AND CONSTRUCTIVISM AS IDENTIFICATORY POSITIONS

Biology and social constructivism as antithetical postulates are, in our vision, identificatory positions and explanatory metaphors that reflect particular relationships between self and other, subject and object. What Wright describes as genetically transmitted, for example, also can be understood as social needs gleaned from social contexts. Is the "biological" press for gene transmission biological, or might it be a "biologization" of social/relational needs, a biological disguise for relatedness? What Vygotsky sees as socially constructed would seem to have some, if only minimal, biological qualities, or else why is it language per se that develops and not a myriad of different communication forms?

Social Darwinism emphasizes the subject, and the constructivist position offers a corresponding antithetical emphasis on object to the question of the extent to which we are a self (a biology) or the extent to which we are comprised of other (the environment). However, what appears to be heterogeneous and individuated is also homogeneous and unified, particularly even at the most basic level of our being. Certain biological research indicates that human beings share 99.9 percent of genetic material with all other humans and 99.6 percent of their active DNA with chimpanzees (Sagan and Druyan, 1992). Thus, it seems that despite superficial differences, we have much more in common with one another than not.

It is hard to argue, given this data, that "other" is not a part of us, and that what we feel is unique to us, is not also a part of another. Yet, we generally prize our unique individuality and certainly value our separateness from chimpanzees. This psychological experience of ourselves as individual and unique is as basic to our existence as is our genetic make-up. Despite its incongruence with genetic "fact," our psychological identity just as strongly constitutes our being as do our genetics. We psychologically have constructed ourselves as unique human individuals, members of a unique species, despite our genetic sameness with each other and with other forms of life.

Whether we experience ourselves as unique, individuated, and self-contained, or as entwined and interdependent with others is a matter of the unconscious identifications and their conscious counterparts that are active at a given moment. Unconscious knowledge of our genetic commonality with others coexists with a conscious experience of difference. Conscious identifications that lean towards difference, unconsciously correspond to disidentifications with sameness. Alternatively, a conscious sense of sameness is preserved by unconsciously ignoring the experience of difference. People are not individuated or interdependent, same or different, they are both; they harbor both identifications simultaneously at different levels of experience, and construct themselves and others through shifts between identification and disidentification. People unconsciously identify as both subjects and objects in a perpetual dialectic dance, and their theories of humankind and of the world are metaphoric representations of such identificatory configurations.

From a multidimensional model of unconscious experience, where symmetrical being provides an unconscious substrate for psychic life, self-other/nature-nurture discriminations are construed as the sequelae of anaclitic translation. The heterogeneous surface structure that appears to be individuated and delineated is linked to a more inclusive homogenous and unformed deep structure, just as the genetic traits that are manifest in any given individual constitute only a fraction of the genetic material available for expression (Sagan and Druyan, 1992). Within a biological context, the potential gene pool exists within individual cells and is manifest in individual physiognomy; within a psychical context, the symmetrical substrate exists within the related unconscious realm and is expressed in identification and relatedness.

POLITICS AND DESIRE

Cultural aspects of human relatedness, as exemplified by problems of race, gender, and class, can be understood as artifacts of anaclitic transformation from states of symmetry, unity, and sameness to states of asymmetry, disunity, and difference. Samuels (1993), a Jungian in the British object relations tradition, discusses human needs for bifurcation and difference, synthesis, and integration as related to an inherently political dimension of unconscious experience. These contradictory needs for division and synthesis generate a basic duality in the human condition, such that there will always be two genders, binary nations, racial dichotomies, and so on. Categories such as boys and girls, masculine and feminine, black and white, poor and rich are socially constructed around Samuels' posited press for bifurcation. Characteristics attributed to one polarity or the other represent the complementary tensions within the individual posed by this inherent duality.

Samuels describes a preexisting link or "primary mutuality" (p. 49) between people that exists on personal, social, and political levels. Individual development is enmeshed with social and political relations and with a political domain in unconscious life. "The individual person leads not only his or her own life, but also the life of the times" (p. 53). According to Samuels, the political is an innate feature of the unconscious and political energy can be transformed into sexuality or aggression. Neither politics, sex, nor aggression are intrinsically superior; involvement with the outer world, in terms of politics and culture, is on par with an interior perspective of the psyche and with interpersonal intimacy. There is a constant articulation between the individual, the private, the subjective and the collective, the social, and the political.

Interestingly, Bettelheim (1989) asserted that the tenets of Freud's theory were an unconscious attempt on Freud's part to master the feelings evoked by the events he was witnessing in the political climate of Austria near the turn of the century. Bettelheim asserts that the theory that Freud created represented a defensive response to the anxiety, fear, and powerlessness that he experienced within the sociopolitical milieu in which he found himself. The intra-psychic focus of classical psychoanalysis was a manifestation of Freud's defensive internalization of the sociopolitical backdrop to his life. What he could not understand or control externally, he could retreat from and manage internally. Considering this hypothesis, the culture of psychoanalysis may have colluded with Freud's defensive emphasis on internal processes, favoring the interior over the exterior.

Social problems of race, gender, and class can be described, from a Kleinian viewpoint, with reference to psychic issues of greed, envy, and persecutory anxiety and in terms of the splitting and projective identification that fit with transformations from similarity to dissimilarity, disintegration to integration. Within the Kleinian concept of the paranoid-schizoid position, the bad or unwanted parts of the self are projected into others to protect the self from experiences of badness, and, equally, from experiences of desire that cannot yet be integrated into the self. The more we split off our internal from our external experience, the more we feel ourselves to be ineluctably different from those on whom we project, the more persecutory anxiety reigns, and the more we are caught in the destructiveness of our own hatred. The softening of the paranoid-schizoid position is in direct correspondence to the degree to which reparative functions operate, allowing for the more depressive functions of empathy and concern to take hold, and diminishing our fears of our own destructiveness and our need to spoil with envy.

Prejudice and Group Identity

Young-Bruehl's (1996) recent critique of prejudice framed the social problems of anti-Semitism, racism, and sexism in terms of what she calls ideologies of desire, which she saw as reactions against political movements toward parity. Formulated in terms of sameness and difference, "ideologies of desire are, generally, backlashes against movements of equality; they are regressive prejudices that reinstate inequalities and distinctions when the force of movements for equality has been registered and (often unconsciously) rejected. . . . Prejudices institutionalize at deeper and more inchoate individual and social or political levels the differences between 'us' and 'them' that movements for equality address" (p. 30).

Within this framework, Young-Bruehl offers a critique of character types (hysterical, narcissistic, obsessional) and their intersection with the ideologies of desire. She attempts to reinstate the importance of character and unconscious motivation to the consideration of economic/material social problems in order to help counteract a pervasive cognitive social learning focus of the American intellectual scene. However, she fails to develop the most interesting idea she presents: that of the flight to difference that marks these ideologies of desire. Instead, she employs an ego-psychological analysis, pairing racism with hysterical prejudice (the other seen as sexually powerful), anti-Semitism with obsessional prejudice (the other seen as polluting with filth), and sexism and homophobia with narcissistic prejudice (the other seen as not-us and therefore less). To some extent, Young-Bruehl embraces the importance of projection (and what she calls the projection theory of prejudice), but she speaks of the contents of projection in ego-psychological terms. Splitting and projections particularly are viewed as applicable to the hysterical character style, and she misses the opportunity to view the problem, in general, as a difficulty in the projective-introjective process and a failure of the depressive position.

In contrast, Alford's (1989) analysis is a Kleinian one. "Groups" he says, "tend to remain stuck at the paranoid-schizoid stage" (p. 84). Group psychology is not identical to individual psychology. Individuals who operate basically within the depressive position, who do not have an over reliance on splitting and extensive projective identification, may operate within the paranoid-schizoid position when identified as a member of the group. Thus, a situation might be imagined in which internal persecutory anxiety is fueled by a group membership which, in valuing the group and devaluing or fearing those outside the group, meets the persecutory experience of otherness in the external world. So, since hate is met with hate, rather than with holding or containment of metabolized affect as it would be in more favorable circumstances, persecutory anxiety is intensified and breeds more hate.

We contend that certain elements in the nature of groups cultivate a paranoid-schizoid ideology. Identification with group membership fosters dissociation; defining the self via others in a group encourages splitting. The process of forming identifications simultaneously fosters the formation of disidentifications with those who do not share that identity. In a group setting, the increased number of participants increases the complexity of the identificatory matrix toward a point of overstimulation at which there is too much complexity to process. The dissociation that is basic to construction of self and other also reduces this increased complexity into a system that is dualistic or dichotomous. What is too much to process is reduced to the least common denominator, a dyadic or dualistic condition. We agree with Samuels (1993) that this dualism may be sewn into the fabric of the human psyche. Originating in the unification of sperm and egg within the body of another, and in the early mother-child dyad, human beings, from conception, continually deal with dialectical shifts from one into two and two into one.

A solution to splitting and the splintering of group ideology into increasingly divisive factions, is what Alford calls reparative reason. Characteristic of the depressive position, reparative reason assists the object in revealing itself, letting the object take the lead rather than constituting our categories of it. Reparative reason is based on the loose symbolic equation, which requires that the subject mourn the loss of identity between a thing and its symbol. This capacity is a hallmark of psychic maturity. The rigid symbolic equation, in contrast, fuses the symbol with the original object and is constituted through primitive projective identification, wherein the relationship to the symbol is one of omnipotent control. The transition to the mode of loose symbolic equations requires a flexibility in which the subject is able to maintain his identification with the original object at the same time that he recognizes or accepts its difference. This capacity to simultaneously differentiate and dedifferentiate from the other is central to subjective relational processes. Reparation and reconciliation, in the Kleininan tradition, is not a utopian project in which socially dichotomized groups (men and women, black and white, rich and poor) reach the highest unity, but one in which a loving connection with objects can be sustained along with an aggressive opposition to them.

The Kleininan dialectic maintains an informative tension between self and other, sameness and difference, inside and outside, the psychic and the social, etc. throughout human experience via projective and introjective identifications. Samuels (1993), in his fundamental concept of collective human experience based upon shared states of nonseparateness, seeks to go beyond the notion of individuality and separateness in a direction consonant with subject-relational premises. He challenges ideas of projective identification that suggest biases in the direction of disconnection or difference. In his words, "The bias is toward throwing and that suggests an empty space between people across which psychic contents are hurled. People are not fundamentally connected in this vision of things; they are momentarily connected when someone plunges something into somebody else. . . . [T]his ignoring of communality and communion in the name of communication is not politically neutral" (p. 276).

However, it is precisely that bias that characterizes the paranoid-schizoid mode of being and that helps clarify the mechanisms through which persons become alien, other, and in persecutory situations, hated and dangerous. Introjective identification and subjective identificatory modes of relating, which embody experiences

of sameness, identity, and obliteration of boundaries, are its counterpart. Politically, the problem lies not in the way in which projective identification is conceptualized, but in the tendency to favor
projective over introjective mechanisms. Kleinian theory leads in
the direction of regarding projective identification as pathological
when it is not balanced by introjective identifications. This very
privileging is definitive of a pathological miring in the paranoid-
schizoid mode of experience, and a failure of restitutive functions
necessary for the preservation of humanity.

Although any experience of otherness can be regarded as a
persecutory mechanism, a splitting of the internal world into
components of me and not-me, based on projection and dissociation of elements of the self into other, we regard class, race, gender and power as particularly pervasive embodiments of split
experience in American culture. Splitting represents an objective
identificatory mode of relating without the counter balance of
subjective identificatory relatedness. This contradiction of ex-
tremes eschews the array of subtleties that lies between the ex-
tremes on both conscious and unconscious levels. The following
clinical and personal examples illustrate our formulations of the
dialectical presence of self and other in cultural and individual
identification.

Power, Class, and Desire: The Poor Little Rich Girl

In the culture of the United States, power tends to be translated into issues of gender or race, and class is commingled with
racial or national identity, but both carry meanings of envy and
desire. Cultural issues regarding power and class are seldom the
direct focus of psychoanalytic work and, quite possibly, less frequently addressed than issues of race or ethnicity. Usually, they
are reduced into terms of individual psychology, while the meaning of individual dynamics more rarely is seen an artifact of culture. However, concrete, personal attributes can come to signify
abstract, political experience. The following case description addresses both sides of this process, the internalization of experiences of class and power into individual symptomatology and

the externalization of individual experience onto sociopolitical position.

Naomi's Patient

Leigh was the beautiful, blond, blue-eyed, sixteen-year-old daughter and only girl in a very wealthy family headed by a politically powerful man who ruled the family with autocratic authority. Objectively, the power in the family rested with him. Leigh entered psychoanalysis when she became seriously anorexic to the point of jeopardizing her life.

Each of Leigh's parents, who were of working-class origins, had lived under conditions of psychological and physical privation during periods of their lives, but rose rapidly into the upper economic echelon in the years immediately preceding their daughter's birth. They became the envied and the desired, and they hoped to put away their own envy and desire by disentangling themselves from their poorer origins. The lifestyle in which Leigh was raised was marked by material excess. Her surroundings were spacious and beautiful, the food presented at meals was expensive and copious, and money was spent lavishly to create an ambiance of quality and taste in all things. Many of the features common in the families of anorexic girls were present in Leigh's family: gender roles were stereotypical; appearances, control, and perfectionism were always important; sexuality was conflictual; hypocrisy and inauthenticity were constant undercurrents.

In spite of (i.e., to spite and despite) their working-class background, Leigh's parents showed little regard for others outside of the wealthier social classes, conveying an attitude of disdain and superiority toward them. Although Leigh's demeanor of refinement and class had a tinge of this same superiority, she consciously rejected their attitudes and distinguished herself from their scorn and arrogance in her attitudes and manner. Leigh felt objectified by her parents as an adornment to their lives, a treasured object of beauty that enhanced their prestige. This objectification left little space for any inner feelings that were incongruent with their image of her.

Outwardly, Leigh *was* the ideal fit for the persona of her family. Beautiful, intelligent, and kind, Leigh carried herself with the gentle grace and sophistication befitting a daughter of privilege. Objectively, the relationship between Leigh and her parents was shaped around a shared, class-defined identity that belied the existence of any privation or impoverishment. Any differences between them were disavowed and obscured by this mutually created image of seamless perfection. Inwardly, however, Leigh felt very different than her parents and different than they perceived her. At this subjective level, their relatedness was constructed around isolation and difference and their similarities were dissociated. Leigh's anorexia created bridges between experiences of difference and sameness between her and her parents, and between the unconscious sense of poverty and powerlessness and the consciously held experience of richness and privilege that permeated her family.

Leigh's self-deprivation symbolized the dissociation of her plenitude and a disidentification from desire. Unconsciously, Leigh needed to move the theme of privation into the foreground of individual and relational experience, to make her inner deprivation known. Through restricting food, she attempted to make private experiences of privation and emptiness concrete and visible. So that she would not be the object of others' desire, so that others would not desire her, Leigh denied herself desire (appetite). She mitigated her fear that the envy and greed of others (including her parents' unconscious envy that she acquired class and privilege just by virtue of her birth) would alienate or destroy her. She assuaged her guilt over partaking of the status and privilege that she did not earn, but that came to her only for being her father's daughter. Leigh could not eat because she already had too much, at the same time that she had never had enough.

In an unconscious effort to expunge those psychic elements that might spoil their identities as people of power and plenty, Leigh's parents created themselves in their own image. Unconsciously they related to Leigh as the object of their own feelings of emotional starvation, poverty, and powerlessness, making her into them, and making themselves match their desired image of class and superiority. Leigh embodied—literally and figuratively—their dissociated deprivation and desire through subjective identificatory relatedness. Her transformation of unconscious feelings into bodily experience paralleled her parents' transformation of their unconscious experience into hers. Leigh became starved, impoverished, and powerless to feed herself. Her anorexia symbolically and concretely expressed the unconscious experience of emotional malnourishment that she shared with her parents.

Hoping to integrate this mutual inner poverty without room in her exterior world to create and experience deprivation, Leigh created a perishing self through self-imposed starvation. She defined herself through the subjectification/introjection of her parents' unconscious and dissociated experience. In an unconscious effort to experience sameness and identity with her parents, Leigh related to them subjectively, making herself into them by introjecting their projections. She became both the poor little rich girl and the rich little poor girl.

Leigh's anorexia and its physical discomforts also signified an unconscious motif of being allied with an impoverished class that encapsulates powerlessness, chronic discomfort, never having enough and barely surviving. Like the underclasses of society, Leigh's power rested in her ability to make visible and undeniable the underbelly of illusions of security, superiority, and privilege. However, despite Leigh's need to disidentify from her parent's class identifications, their ability and willingness to provide virtually unlimited financial support enabled her to have the analysis necessary to avoid hospitalization, gain and maintain weight, and move away from her anorexic identity. Their support represented their unconscious hope for and participation in the melding of their own fragmented experience via their daughter's illness and analysis. For Leigh, the duality between her struggle with class identifications and her reliance on her family's wealth symbolized her strivings to integrate her poverty with her plenitude.

Black, White, and Shades of . . . Gray?:
Racial Identifications Rejected and Embraced

Despite its institutionalization in our culture, racism, on a psychic level, may be regarded more as a projective process than an ideology, existing more on an irrational and unconscious level than on a logical and rational one. Racial differences depend on the definition attributed to them by the other; they have no essential substance of their own. The emptiness of racial categories makes them an easy container for projective meaning. Black-white difference carries the effects of culture, class, and nationality, and not simply color (e.g., Rustin, 1991). In the United States and in more blatantly colonial European societies, especially, the opposition of black and white is the repository for intensely personal dissociated self-experiences. The examples presented reflect differences between objective/projective and subjective/introjective modes and identifications regarding racial distinctions, and highlight the potential for racial categories both to reflect and define the experienced self.

Karen's Father

A shopkeeper who was more properly petit bourgeois than nondescriptively middle class, my father was also a failed entertainer. He had relinquished a career as a French horn player for a career in professional baseball, only to injure his shoulder just as the major leagues were reportedly in his grasp. His racism might easily be attributed to the shared attitude of his provincial, struggling middle-American subculture, or to the economic insecurities of the petit bourgeois. I see it, however, better described as a projected self-contempt at his own failed celebrity status, and his envy of those who succeeded. My memories of being attacked by his racism include his fury with me for supporting black rock-and-roll and popular performers by buying their records. *Good Golly, Miss Molly* wasn't exactly a Mozart horn concerto.

At the age of eleven, I was aware that my father felt that my taste in music was a personal act of betrayal of him. From the perspective of an adult, his envy of my interest in "their" music and of my support of "their" success stands in clear relief to his own failure to have made it against all odds. Throughout his life, he maintained a racist ideology that served as a container for his own sense of disenfranchisement and failure. Nevertheless, along with his racism, he formed affectionate ties with particular black men and women by making individual exceptions.

As our neighborhood became "inner city" throughout the sixties, and more of our neighbors came from the black middle class, my father became genuinely fond of many of his black neighbors. One became his personal physician and he relied on many others for support and advice. During the racial rebellions of the 1960s, the white-owned businesses along our street were trashed for several blocks; all, that is, except my father's. My father sat up all night in his store with the lights on, a shotgun on the counter, and our next-door neighbor, Kathryn, beside him. Kathryn, a black woman who wielded a great deal of power in the local black community, spent the night on the street trying to contain people's frustration and rage and, not incidentally, protecting my father. In his later life his racism took an increasingly bimodal form, simultaneously coexisting with his love and admiration for Kathryn, Doc Bodie, and other black individuals.

Naomi's Mother

Like Karen, I grew up in a middle-class integrated neighborhood that became largely black following the racial discord of the 1960s. My mother, a Caucasian woman now eighty years old, was married for fifty years to my father, a black man from a racially mixed family who died recently. My mother had been raised in an educated, middle-class, Midwestern family. She was the second of two daughters, the first of whom was seriously injured as a toddler at the time my mother was born, and who required extensive care and attention for many months. In relation to her sister's needs in those early years, my mother developed a gentle patience, slowness to anger, and a tendency to be self-effacing. She is kind, loyal, and intelligently perceptive. She has a gracious spirit balanced by fortitude and independence of mind that I have increasingly admired and appreciated over time.

Over the years, my mother developed close friends who were black and became known and accepted by the black community in which she lived. As the years of her marriage to my father passed, my mother began to look much like my father's sisters—in particular, his favorite sister, Naomi. While there were no specific features that gave her the appearance of being black, she developed an intangible quality about her presence that made her easily mistakable for a black woman of light complexion. As she has aged, my mother has come to identify more and more with the issues, feelings, and experiences poor blacks often face and to experience herself more like them than like a member of the middle-class white population of which she would technically be said to belong. Her black identifications are sometimes an irritant to me, for complicated reasons that concern my struggle with the conflictual identifications that came with being a biracial child of the 1950s and 1960s. Between us, this tension also concerns our mutual and individual integration of my father.

In her "blackness," my mother maintains an unconscious tie with my father and his history, and with their life together. Her black identifications represent the introjection of qualities of people that she has loved and valued, at the same time that it represents an expression of her need to take a back seat to her sister in her early years. She has immersed herself in that which is not-her, making the non-self into the self through subjective modes of relating and introjective identification, creating her own being.

Gendered Selves: What Are Little Girls Made Of?

The contemporary debate over gender focuses on the question of essentialism, on whether innate, universal, and immutable differences exist between men and women, or whether masculinity and femininity are culturally constructed. The essentialist argument that biology is psychic destiny is a familiar one, exemplified by the notions that girls like to play with dolls and build enclosures, while boy prefer trucks and build towers. The less familiar social constructionist view sees masculinity and femininity as socially symbolized and gender ideology as producing, rather than produced by, notions of the biological dichotomy between men and women. However, explanatory models of essentialism or constructionism, like those of nature or nurture, are opposing poles of a false dichotomy that does not consider the dialectical relation of polarized experience or the qualititative nuances that occupy the intermediate space between polarities. The following personal vignettes were selected to illustrate gender differences as both creating and being creations of the experienced self.

Karen's Daughter

Chloë, at three and a half, had experiences with both male and female public restrooms, since her father and I shared in accompanying her on trips to the restroom. One mens' restroom in a hotel had bright yellow urinals. Pointing to the urinals, Chloë looked up at her father and said, "I'm going to use one of these like you when I grow up, but mine's going to be pink."

At about this same age, Chloë was also fascinated with video games, whereas I am quite horrified by their relentless and numbing violence. I tried to steer her toward baby Pacman games and my preference for the oral incorporative mode. At one particular video arcade at a highway rest stop, she wanted to play a game where a gun blasted rather real representations of people out of existence. When I responded with unmodulated affect, "Absolutely not! Under no circumstances! That's disgusting," Chloë amused herself with milder entertainment. As we were walking toward the car, she turned to me and said "Mommy, tomorrow I'm going to be a boy and then I can play that game." She looked at me out of the corner of her eye, as if to catch the expression on my face, and burst out laughing.

These interchanges were play, expressions of Chloë's capacity to play with symbols in ways that enabled her to move between subject and object experiences, so that new ways of being in the world could be forged. Her playful exchange of gender identifications lived on the border between that which was subjectively experienced (Chloë as boy and girl) and that which was objectively perceived (Chloë as girl, not boy).

Naomi's Daughter

Clara, between the ages of three and nine, was a very extroverted, aggressive tomboy, despite her many feminine wiles and sensual, physical nature. She reveled in using "bad" language, preferred shooting games, basketball, and learning to play the electric guitar, rejected dolls, and refused to wear a dress or any "girl" clothing (i.e., clothing with hearts, flower, rainbows, ruffles or that was colored pink or purple). For those years, I dressed her in boys' t-shirts and jeans, and had to buy her a boys' bicycle because all the girls bicycles in her size were the dreaded pink or purple. At the same time, Clara was very drawn to men and to sexuality, and she could be very seductive in a surprisingly sophisticated way that was very unlike me.

Our immediate family consists of myself and my older child—a boy, Philip—who is very shy, introspective, mild mannered, and seen by others as unusually composed and mature. While he is masculine in demeanor, he does not have the interests or expansive, driving energy that are often evident in boys of his age. I am the sole parent of my children and I did not have a close romantic or sexual involvement with a man during Clara's early years. Nor did Clara have a close relationship with a male paternal figure. Yet, in our family, it is Clara who exhibits both masculine energy and sexuality. Her tomboyish aggressiveness and sexual/sensuality express her subjective and introjective identifications with an unconscious layer of our family, while expressing her disidentifications with external characteristics of myself and Philip.

Moreover, the fantasized paternal figure that classical theory would predict a girl would invoke in the absence of a father, has been my father for Clara. This would not be surprising except for the fact that Clara only saw him three times in her life—at three weeks of age, at age one, and at age two—since he died before her fourth birthday. At their last visit together, Clara, my extremely active two-year-old who never was still, sat on the couch next to my ailing father for a full afternoon without leaving, talking to him in baby speech that he could not understand, but delighted in. Although no one in the family speaks of my father excessively, Clara has cried about his death numerous times over a period of years, keeps his picture by her bedside, and states that she "feels like him and misses him." In fact, her defiant spirit is like his and he would have adored her.

Clara's connection to my father is reminiscent of my connection with him. He cherished and took great pleasure in me, and, I believe, understood some very deep-seated and unexpressed feelings of mine. Although we did not have particularly much to converse about over later years, I felt close to him. My relationship with my father during my early childhood holds some of the best memories of my life. The psychical father that Clara created for herself was a shared father. She constructed him largely through her identifications with unconscious, or covert, representations in me that were my father's legacy. This sharing of my father represented her subjective connection with my experience as a young child with my father, and provided a positive identificatory milieu in which she could develop her own femininity.

Culture in the Related Unconscious

In the related unconscious, the political and the personal both reflect and are reflected in the infinite dimensions by which people are psychical beings. Cultural divisions are formulated around dissimilitude and objectification, but anchored in symmetry, sameness and subjectivity. We have selected class, race and gender, to illustrate our formulations about culture, yet, these formulations are also applicable to issues such as nationalism and religious or political prejudice. The phrase "discriminated against" catches the emptiness that Samuels (1993) described regarding cultural or political divisions. Groups are distinguished (discriminated) by their contrast to something else (against). Whether these divisions are essential or constructed, natural or nurtured is a false controversy. The push to construct experience is essential to human nature and the essence of being human constructs experience.

Notions of both individual and culture are fashioned by the intricate complex of identifications and disidentifications that reverberate throughout human experience, generating external and internal experience and object-relating and subject-relating. Subject relations in cultural experience comprise the unity that all people share, the unconscious modes in which we *are* our (br)others (and sisters) and the sameness against which objective categories are defined and cultural distinctions acquire meaning. Individuals become social beings at the juncture of asymmetrical multiplicity and symmetrical inclusiveness, and the dialectic between these modes forms individual and cultural experience. "Man being part of the world reflects, in some way, the structure of the world . . . man cannot but see the macrocosmos only as he himself is made" (Matte-Blanco, 1975, pp. 389–90).

Epilogue

N.R.: In one of my earliest memories (from about age two or three), I am sitting alone, fascinated by the image on the jacket of a childrens' book. On the cover of that book was a picture of a girl reading the same book with the same picture on its cover of a girl reading the same book with the same cover—in endless refrain. I recall that I was totally immersed in this image, experiencing myself going deeper and deeper into it through layers and layers of imaginary girls holding imaginary books. For me, *Subject Relations* began with that book; it is only fitting that it ends with that book as well.

The same mesmerizing fascination, tinged with vertigo, that I experienced looking at that book cover I have felt organizing the ideas in this volume. The mode of thinking it has entailed is difficult to convey verbally or organize logically with clarity. It is circuitous and endlessly reverberates. Like escaping a whirlpool to return to the surface, or perhaps like stepping off a Mobius strip, one must move along for awhile and then strike out decisively in order to escape its hypnotic pull. The point of departure is arbitrary, but imperative. This book and the culmination of this phase of my relationship with Karen come to a close with that same wrenching determination. Neither endings are easy, only necessary.

Subject Relations is my attempt to make sense of that early experience, to use all the words and intellect that my subsequent years have given me in order to create understanding and sense out of sensibility. What I have come away with is the understanding that this is not really possible. I now have words to complement experience, I have some framework in which words and sensibility fit together, and I have metamorphasized from a little girl holding a book to an adult writing one. Yet, really and truly, I still feel myself to be that first little girl holding the book, mesmerized by the infinitude implied in that book jacket.

K.L.: I have a similar, if somewhat later, memory at age five or six. I am sitting alone in my room imagining infinity in the form of innumerable containers each holding a diminishing, more minute image of the previous one. This experience was simultaneously of growing smaller and smaller, while exponentially enlarging, much as if Alice were fanning herself with the White Rabbit's fan and eating the caterpillar's mushroom at once.

Such experience simultaneously expresses theories of the contraction and expansion of the universe in a bilogical mode. The attempt to apprehend the thing that holds itself infinitely, or that fractures endlessly, is a human dilemma that presents itself perhaps most viscerally and vividly to the young mind. Naomi's calmer, more held and articulated early impression echoes my own more kinesthetic and inchoate early sense of the eliding reality of infinitude.

These dual memories are one manifestation of the ways in which we resonate with each other, and they symbolize the deepening of our relationship that is reflected by the content and writing of this book. Together we have explored our shared fascination with the infinite. We have called upon our unconscious experiences, the vicissitudes of our relatedness, and our common psychoanalytic bent to create *Subject Relations: Unconscious Experience and Relational Psychoanalysis*. We have worked to integrate that mutual early experience of infinite reverberation, and, in putting it into words, to live it and be lived by it.

REFERENCES

Abrams, D. (1992). "The Dream's Mirror." *Contemporary Psychoanalysis, 28*(1), 50–71.

Abse, D. (1976). "Delusional Identity and the Double." *Psychiatry, 39*(2), 163–75.

Adler, M. (1992). *Great Ideas: A Lexicon of Western Thought.* New York: MacMillan.

Alford, C. F. (1989). *Melanie Klein and Critical Social Theory.* New Haven, CT: Yale University Press.

Alvarez, A. (1988). "Beyond the Pleasure Principle: Some Preconditions for Thinking Through Play." *Journal of Child Psychotherapy, 14*(2), 1–13.

Anzieu, D. (1989). *The Skin Ego: A Psychoanalysis of the Self.* New Haven, CT: Yale University Press.

Arlow, J. (1960). "Fantasy Systems in Twins." *Psychoanalytic Quarterly, 29*, 175–99.

Aron, L. (1990). "One-Person and Two-Person Psychologies and the Method of Psychoanalysis." *Psychoanalytic Psychology. 17*, 475–85.

——. (1996). *A Meeting of Minds: Mutuality and Psychoanalysis.* Hillsdale, NJ: Analytic Press.

Balint, M. (1968). *The Basic Fault.* New York: Brunner-Mazel.

Benjamin, J. (1988). *The Bonds of Love: Psychoanalysis, Feminism, and the Problem of Domination.* New York: Pantheon.

——. (1991). "Father and Daughter: Identification with Difference— A Contribution to Gender Heterodoxy. *Psychoanalytic Dialogues, 1*(3), 277–99.

Bettelheim, B. (1982). *Freud and Man's Soul.* New York: Vintage Books.

——. (1989). *Freud's Vienna and Other Essays.* New York: Alfred A. Knopf.

Bion, W. (1959). "Attacks on Linking." *International Journal of Psychoanalysis, 40,* 308–15.

——. (1967). "The Imaginary Twin." In *Second Thoughts: Selected Thoughts on Psychoanalysis.* New York: Basic Books.

——. (1977). "On a Quotation from Freud." In P. Hartocollis (ed.), *Borderline Personality Disorder: The Concept, the Syndrome, the Patient.* New York: International Universities Press.

Bleandonu, G. (1994). *Wilfred Bion.* New York: Guilford Press.

Bohm, D. (1980). *Wholeness and the Implicate Order.* London: Routledge & Kegan Paul.

Bollas, C. (1992). "Unconscious Communication and the Communication of the Unconscious." Paper presented at the Annual Small Conference in Psychoanalysis, Naples, Florida.

Bucheimer, A. (1987). "Memory: Pre-Verbal and Verbal." In T. Verny (ed.), *Pre- and Peri-natal Psychology: An Introduction.* New York: Human Sciences Press.

Capra, F. (1982). *The Turning Point.* New York: Bantam Books.

Carstairs, K. (1992). "Paranoid-Schizoid or Symbiotic?" *International Journal of Psychoanalysis, 73,* 71–85.

Cavell, M. (1989a). "Interpretation, Psychoanalysis and the Philosophy of the Mind." *Journal of the American Psychoanalytic Association, 37,* 859–79.

——. (1989b). "Solipsism and Community: Two Concepts on Mind in Philosophy and Psychoanalysis." *Psychoanalysis and Contemporary Thought. 12,* 587–613.

Chamberlain, D. (1987). "Consciousness at Birth." In T. Verny (ed.), *Pre- and Peri-Natal Psychology: An Introduction*. New York: Human Sciences Press.

———. (1990). "The Expanding Boundaries of Memory." *Pre- and Peri-Natal Psychology Journal, 4*(3), 171–89.

Chodorow, N. (1978). *The Reproduction of Mothering: Psychoanalysis and the Sociology of Gender*. Berkeley: University of California Press.

———. (1989). *Feminism and Psychoanalytic Theory*. New Haven, CT: Yale University Press.

———. (1996). "Reflections on the Authoritiy of the Past in Psychoanalytic Thinking." *Psychoanalytic Quarterly, 65*, 32–51.

Civin, M. and K. Lombardi. (1990). "The Preconscious and Potential Space." *Psychoanalytic Review, 77*(4), 573–85.

Clayton, V. (1982). "Wisdom and Intelligence: The Nature and Function of Knowledge in Later Years." *International Journal of Aging and Human Development, 15*(4), 315–21.

Dittman-Kohli, F. and Baltes, P. (1990). "Toward a Neofunctionalist Conception of Adult Intellectual Development: Wisdom as a Prototypical Case of Intellectual Growth." In C. Alexander and E. Langer (eds.), *Higher Stages of Human Development*. (pp. 54–78), New York: Oxford University Press.

Donovan, D. (1989). "The Paraconscious." *Journal of the American Academy of Psychoanalysis, 17*(2), 232–51.

Eisenbud, J. (1970). *PSI and Psychoanalysis*. Orlando, Florida: Grune.

Eliot, T.S. (1963). *Collected Poems 1909–1962*. New York: Harcourt, Brace and World.

Fairbairn, W.R.D. (1952). *Psychoanalytic Studies of the Personality*. London: Routledge & Kegan Paul.

Feffer, M. (1982). *The Structure of Freudian Thought*. New York: International Universities Press.

Ferenczi, S. (1915). "Psychogenic Anomalies of Voice Production." In *Further Contributions to the Theory and Technique of Psychoanalysis*. New York: Brunner/Mazel.

Fourcher, L. (1992). "Interpreting the Relative and Absolute Unconscious." *Psychoanalytic Dialogues, 2*(3), 317–29.

Freud, S. (1909). "The Interpretation of Dreams." In James Strachey (ed.), *Standard Edition, 5*, 382–404, London: Hogarth Press.

——. (1912). "The Dynamics of Transference." In *Standard Edition*, *12*, 97–108.

——. (1915). "A Metapsychological Supplement to the Theory of Dreams." In *Standard Edition*, *14*, 222–35.

——. (1916–17). "Some Thoughts on Development and Regression— aetiology." In *Standard Edition*, *16*, 339–57.

——. (1919). "The Uncanny." *Standard Edition*, *17*, 217–56.

——. (1923). "The Ego and the Id." *Standard Edition*, *19*, 12–66.

——. (1926). "Inhibitions, Symptoms and Anxiety." In *Standard Edition*, *20*, 77–175.

Freud, W. E. (1987). "Pre-Natal Attachment and Bonding." In T. Verny (ed.), *Pre- and Peri-Natal Psychology: An Introduction*. New York: Human Sciences Press.

Gerson, S. (1995). "The Analyst's Subjectivity and the Relational Unconscious." Paper presented at the Spring Meeting of the American Psychological Association Division 39.

Gilligan, C. (1982). *In a Different Voice: Psychological Theory and Women's Development*. Cambridge, MA: Harvard University Press.

Groddeck, G. (1923/1949). *The Book of the It*. New York: Alfred A. Knopf.

Guntrip, H. (1968). *Schizoid Phenomena, Object Relations and the Self*. London: Hogarth Press.

Hegel, G. W. (1817/1965). *The Logic of Hegel*. New York: Oxford University Press.

Hinshelwood, R. D. (1991). *A Dictionary of Kleinian Thought*. London: Free Association Books.

Hirsch, I. and Roth, J. (1995). "Changing Conceptions of the Unconscious." *Contemporary Psychoanalysis*, *31*, (2), 263–76.

Jordan, J. N., A. G. Kaplan, J. B. Miller, , I. P. Striver, and J. L. Surrey. (1991). *Women's Growth in Connection*. New York: Guilford Press.

Kant, I. (1781/1965). *Critique of Pure Reason*. New York: St. Martin's Press.

Kern, J. (1978). "Countertransference and Spontaneous Screens: An Analyst Studies His Own Visual Images." *Journal of the American Psychoanalytic Association*, *26*, 21–47.

Klaus, M. and J. Kennell. (1976). *Maternal-Infant Bonding*. Saint Louis, MO: Mosley.

Klein, M. (1946). "Some Schizoid Mechanisms." In *Envy and Gratitude.*, New York: Delacorte Press.

———. (1955). "On Identification." In *Envy and Gratitude.* New York: Delacorte Press.

———. (1957). "Envy and Gratitude." In *Envy and Gratitude.* New York: Delacorte Press.

———. (1959). "Our Adult World and Its Roots in Infancy." In *Envy and Gratitude.* New York: Delacorte Press.

Kohut, H. (1971). *The Analysis of the Self.* New York: International Universities Press.

———. (1977). *The Restoration of the Self.* New York: International Universities Press.

Kosok, M. (1970). "The Dialectics of Nature." *Telos, 6,* 47–103.

Laing, R. D. (1976). *The Facts of Life.* New York: Pantheon Books.

Langer, S. (1966). *Mind: An Essay in Human Feeling.* Baltimore, MD: John Hopkins University Press.

Likierman, M. (1988) "Maternal Love and Positive Projective Identification." *Journal of Child Psychotherapy, 14(2),* 29–46.

Lombardi, K. and N. Rucker. (1991). "Parallel Dreams as a Form of Transitional Relatedness with the Silent Patient." Paper presented at the Spring Meeting of the American Psychological Association Division 39, Chicago, Illinois.

Lyons-Ruth, K. (1991). "Rapprochement or Approchement: Mahler's Theory Reconsidered from the Vantage Point of Recent Research on Early Attachment Relationships." *Psychoanalytic Psychology, 8(1),* 1–23.

Mahler, M., F. Pine, and A. Bergman. (1975). *The Psychological Birth of the Human Infant.* New York: Basic Books.

Maizels, N. (1990). "The Destructive Confounding of Intra-uterine and Post-uterine Life as a Factor Opposing Emotional Development." *Melanie Klein and Object Relations, 8(2),* 31–47.

Matte-Blanco, I. (1975). *The Unconscious as Infinite Sets.* London: Duckworth.

———. (1988). *Thinking, Feeling, and Being.* London and New York: Routledge.

McDougall, J. (1978). "Primitive Communication and the Use of Countertransference." *Contemporary Psychology, 19,* 173–209.

Mitchell, S. (1984). "Object Relations and the Developmental Tilt." *Contemporary Psychoanalysis, 20*(4), 473–499.

——. (1993). *Hope and Dread in Psychoanalysis.* New York: Basic Books.

Montague, M. (1950). "Constitutional and Prenatal Factors in Infant and Child Health." In M.J. Senn (ed.) *Symposium on the Healthy Personality,* 148–69. New York: Macy Foundation.

Murray (1995) "On Objects, Transference and Two-Person Psychology: A Critique of the New Seduction Theory." *Psychoanalytic Psychology, 12*(1), 31–42.

Newirth, J. (1996). "Psychoanalysis and the Unconscious: The Phoenix Rising from the Ashes." Paper presented at the spring meeting of the American Psychological Association Division 39 (Psychoanalysis), New York.

Ogden, T. H. (1992a). "The Dialectically Constituted/Decentered Subject of Psychoanalysis": I. The Freudian Subject. *International Journal of Psychoanalysis, 73,* 517–26.

——. (1992b). "The Dialectically Constituted/Decentered Subject of Psychoanalysis": II. The Contributions of Klein and Winnicott. *International Journal of Psychoanalysis, 73,* 613–26.

——. (1994). *Subjects of Analysis.* New Jersey: Jason Aronson Press.

Oliner, M. (1988). *Cultivating Freud's Garden in France.* New Jersey: Jason Aronson Press.

Ortmeyer, D. (1970). "The We-Self of Identical Twins." *Contemporary Psychoanalysis, 6*(2), 124–42.

Paul, M. (1989). "Notes on the Primordial Development of the Perinatal Transference." *Melanie Klein and Object Relations, 7*(2), 43–69.

——. (1990). "Studies on the Phenomenon of Mental Pressure." *Melanie Klein and Object Relations,* 8(2), 7–29.

Piontelli, A. (1989). "A study on twins before and after birth." *International Review of Psychoanalysis, 16*(4), 413–26.

——. (1992). *From Fetus to Child: An Observational Study.* New York: Routledge.

Ploye, P. (1973). "Does Prenatal Mental Life Exist?" *International Journal of Psychoanalysis,* 54, 241–46.

Racker, H. (1968). *Transference and Countertransference.* Connecticut: International Universities Press.

Rank, O. (1925/1971). *The Double*. (H. Tucker, ed. & trans.) North Carolina: University of North Carolina Press.

Roiphe, H., and E. Galenson. (1971). "The Impact of Early Sexual Discovery on Mood, Defensive Organization and Symbolization." *Psychoanalytic Study of the Child*, 26, 195–216.

Roland, A. (1988). *In Search of Self in India and Japan*. Princeton: Princeton University Press.

Rottman, G. (1974). "Untersuchungen uber Eiunstellungen zur Schwanger-schaft und zur Fotalen Entwicklung." In G. H. Graber (ed.) *Pranatale Psychologie* (pp. 60–87). Munich: Kindler Verlag.

Rucker, N. (1981). "Capacities for Integration, Oedipal Ambivalence and Imaginary Companions." *American Journal of Psychoanalysis*, 41(2), 129–37.

———. (1994). "Exploratory Thoughts on Wisdom, Intimacy, and Analytic Relatedness." *American Journal of Psychoanalysis*, 54(1), 77–85.

Rustin, M. (1991). *The Good Society and the Inner World: Psychoanalysis, Politics, and Culture*. London: Verso.

Sagan, C. & Druyan, A. (1992). *Shadows of Forgotten Ancestors*. New York: Random House.

Samuels, A. (1993). *The Political Psyche*. London and New York: Routledge.

Schepper-Hughes, N. (1992). *Death without Weeping: The Violence of Everyday Life in Brazil*. Berkeley, California: University of California Press.

Schwartz, A. (1993). "Thoughts on the Construction of Maternal Relationships." *Psychoanalytic Psychology*, 10(3), 331–44.

Searles, H. (1955). "The Informational Value of the Supervisor's Emotional Experience." *Psychiatry*, 18, 135–46.

———. (1960). *The Nonhuman Environment in Normal Development and in Schizophrenia*. New York: International Universities Press.

———. (1979). *Countertransference and Related Subjects*. New York: International Universities Press.

Shlain, L. (1991). *Art and Physics*. New York: William Morrow & Co.

Stern, D. (1985). *The Interpersonal World of the Infant*. New York: Basic Books.

Stolorow, R. D., B. Brandcraft, and G. E. Atwood. (1987). *Psychoanalytic Treatment: An Intersubjective Approach*. New Jersey: Analytic Press.

Sullivan, B. (1989). *Psychotherapy Grounded in the Feminine Principle*. Illinois: Chiron Publications.

Sullivan, H. S. (1953). *The Interpersonal Theory of Psychiatry*. New York: W. W. Norton.

Verny, T. (ed.) (1987). *Pre- and Perinatal Psychology: An Introduction*. New York: Human Sciences Press.

Viderman, S. (1980). "The Subject-Object Relation and the Problem of Desire." In S. Lebovici and D. Widlocher (eds.), *Psychoanalysis in France*. New York: International Universities Press.

Vygotsky, L. (1978). *Mind in Society: The Development of Higher Psychological Processes*. New York: International Universities Press.

Warren, M. (1961). "The Significance of Visual Images During the Analytic Session." *Journal of the American Psychoanalytic Association*, 9, 504–18.

Whyte, R. (1991). "Giving and Taking: The Foetal-Maternal Juncture as a Prototype and Precursor of Object Relations." *British Journal of Psychotherapy, 7*(3), 221–29.

Wilner, W. (1975). "The Nature of Intimacy." *Contemporary Psychoanalysis*, 11(2), 206–26.

——. (1991). "Unusual Unconscious Communications and Enactments: Illustration and Exploration." Paper presented at the spring meeting of the American Psychological Association Division 39 (Psychoanalysis), Chicago, Illinois.

——. (1996a) "Faith and the Analytic Use of Unconscious Experience." Paper presented at the spring meeting of the American Psychological Association Division 39 (Psychoanalysis), New York.

——. (1996b). "Dreams and the Wholistic Nature of Interpersonal Psychoanalytic Experience." Unpublished manuscript.

Wilson, A. (1995). "Mapping the Mind in Relational Psychoanalysis: Some Critiques, Questions, and Conjectures." *Psychoanalytic Psychology, 12*(1), 9–30.

Winnicott, D. W. (1949). "Birth Memories, Birth Trauma, and Anxiety." In *Collected Papers: Through Paediatrics to Psychoanalysis*. New York: Basic Books.

——. (1954). "Withdrawal and Regression." In *Collected Papers: Through Paediatrics to Psychoanalysis*. New York: Basic Books.

——. (1963) "Communicating and Not Communicating Leading to a Study of Certain Opposites." In *The Maturational Processes and the Facilitating Environment.* New York: International Universities Press.

——. (1965). *The Maturational Processes and the Facilitating Environment.* New York: International Universities Press.

——. (1988) "Birth experience." In *Human Nature.* New York: Schocken Books.

Wolstein, B. (1982). "The Psychoanalytic Theory of Unconscious Psychic Experience." *Contemporary Psychoanalysis, 14*(3), 412–37.

——. (1993). "Sandor Ferenczi and the American Interpersonal Relationship: History and Personal Reflections." In L. Harris (ed.) *The Legacy of Sandor Ferenczi.* New Jersey: Analytic Press.

Wright, R. (1994). *The Moral Animal.* New York: Pantheon Books.

Young-Bruehl, E. (1996). *The Anatomy of Prejudices.* Cambridge, MA: Harvard University Press.

Zucker, H. (1989). "Premises of Interpersonal Theory." *Psychoanalytic Psychology,* 6(4), 401–19.

APPENDIX

A SUMMARY OF SELECTED CONSTRUCTS FROM MATTE-BLANCO'S MODEL OF THE UNCONSCIOUS AS INFINITE SETS

The mode of symmetry: Guided by principles of mathematical set theory that tend toward indivisibility and inclusion. A symmetrical relation is one whose converse is identical to it. (Andy likes Jane; Jane likes Andy.) Symmetry is ruled by such nonlinear qualities as timelessness, spacelessness, and the absence of negation, and is more experiential than cognitive. Unity, homogeneity, sameness prevail. (Examples: 1) A male patient dreams of delivering a newborn baby that speaks fluently, knowing in the dream that he was never pregnant; 2) A psychotic woman who was named Louisa Jeanine Hall (actual name changed) after her mother, Jeanine, writes "Lou is a Jeanine Hall," symbolizing her delusion of being her mother and indicating the psychical expansion of her mother as an individual into a class of Jeanine Halls.)

The mode of asymmetry: Guided by principles of Aristotelian logic wherein linear and hierarchical properties of time, space, and movement rule. An asymmetrical relation is one in which its converse is not identical to it. (Carol is carrying Jenny; Jenny is being carried by Carol.) Cognition and thought are made possible by asymmetrical logic. Limits, difference, and heterogeneity prevail. (Examples: 1) conceptualization of objects in the physical world [next to, before, smaller than, etc.]; 2) the scientific method.)

Anaclitic translation or the unfolding function: Links the asymmetrical and the symmetrical modes, continually transforming internal and external experience. Unfolding or anaclitic translation allows pieces of symmetry to be glimpsed asymmetrically by reflecting symmetrical material in an asymmetrical mode, but the fullness of symmetry always escapes translation. Unfolding works in a manner contradictory to repression by pushing unconscious symmetrical material towards the realm of more conscious asymmetrical thought. (Example: A patient in the midst of a deeply psychotic episode has the delusion of being a bear-man in which he is, in his mind, completely a man and a bear at the same time. In a less psychotic state, he has trouble describing this experience. In trying to do so, he describes himself as feeling sometimes like a man and sometimes like a bear, a more differentiated experience than that of a bear-man. He shifts the undifferentiated [symmetrical] dream experience of bear-man into a differentiated, spatial-temporal [asymmetrical] one, but the richness of the bear-man experience is compromised.)

Bivalent logic: An asymmetrical characteristic represented by either-or relations. (Example: The statement: "He is sad, not angry," implies that one can only be sad or angry, not both.)

Bilogic: The mixing of asymmetrical logic and symmetrization. When a bivalently logical sequence might be expected, but symmetrization is inserted, then there is a bilogical structure. The asymmetrical relation is "ignored" in favor of more symmetrical logic. Bilogical structures relinquish some of their asymmetrical consistency through symmetrization. (Example: 1) "Hank is just like his brothers." Hank, who could be differentiated from his brothers, instead is presented as undifferentiated from them, as identical with the more inclusive class of "his brothers". Their [asymmetrical] differences are overlooked and their perceived [symmetrical] sameness is endorsed; 2) A psychotic patient says, "I have my father's nose," meaning that she and her father actually share the same nose. The psychotic meaning of this seemingly ordinary statement is a symmetrization.)

Bimodality: The coexistence of symmetrical and asymmetrical modes, with each simultaneously expressed in the same piece of reality. All parts of a bimodal structure must have at least one commonality, allowing it to be both whole and unique. This is not interpenetration, nor is it cooperation (as it might be in bilogic); there is no insertion of symmetry, only the coexistence of dual relations. Consistency is maintained. (Example: The concept of "a pet" combines many qualities and is both distinct from [asymmetry] and identical with [symmetry] other pets. "Pet," in this regard, contains both asymmetrical and symmetrical relations and thus is bimodally structured.)

Bilogical stratification: The various strata of the mind are differentiated conceptually according to the degree of symmetrization. The degree of symmetry or asymmetry ranges from more superficial to deeper levels of the mind. Human psychical experience is formulated in terms of an infinite series of strata in which the capacity to recognize differences declines as the degree of symmetrization increases. At the symmetrical extreme are indivisibility and infinity; at the asymmetrical extreme are disintegration and fragmentation. Matte-Blanco describes five strata that shift toward increasing symmetry, although there can be an infinite number. (In this book, the terms dimensions and layers are used interchangeably with strata, but they are not Matte-Blanco's terms.)

1) Bivalent thinking is the logic of conscious awareness of discrete objects represented by either-or relations. Realm of delimited, asymmetrical thought.

2) Bivalent thinking still obtains, but with bilogical structures emerging. Realm of affect, symbolism, metaphor.

3) Different classes are identical, but parts of the class are always taken as the whole. Realm of prejudice, idealization, hyperbole, sentimentality, etc.

4) Classes are symmetrized, becoming more inclusive. Only some class differentiation remains.

5) Tends toward mathematical indivisibility and full inclusion of classes with each other. Thinking is greatly impaired. At the symmetrical limit, which is hypothetical and cannot be reached in actuality, an endless number of things becomes only one thing and mental activity is prohibited.

NAME INDEX

SUBJECT INDEX

achronicity, 67–68
affiliative relatedness, 117, 120, 124–27, 129–30
antinomy, 16, 19
asymmetry, 9, 13–20, 26, 28, 30, 32–33, 37, 43, 45–47, 49, 57–58, 62, 64, 66, 70, 72–79, 82, 84–89, 102, 118–124, 126–27, 129, 131, 135, 137–43, 147, 149, 151, 165, 179–80
autistic-contiguous, 62

bilogical, 15–18, 168, 179–80
bimodality, 15, 17, 149, 161, 180
bivalent, 15–17, 149, 179–80
British Middle School, 4, 91, 106, 111

Cartesian dualism, 7
catch experience, 48–49, 56, 59
cathexis, 62, 76, 91–92

class, 144, 151–52, 156–60, 165, 180, 181
classical theory, 1–3, 5, 14, 60–61, 64, 90
  classical formulations, 6
  classical psychoanalysis, 23, 35, 56, 66, 76, 80, 112, 152
  drive theory, 2–4, 6, 62, 103–05, 107, 146
communion, 4, 31, 33, 46, 56–57, 131, 155
complementary identification, 28–30, 45, 57, 119–20, 123–27, 129–30, 138
concordant identification, 28–30, 45, 57–58, 119–20, 123–27, 129–30, 138
conscious, 2, 4, 6–7, 13–14, 16, 23
  reflective, 8–9
correspondant phenomena, 25–27, 32

maternal functions
    mother-child, 20, 31, 58, 73, 76,
        79, 86, 104, 109, 111–2, 115
    mother-daughter, 108
metapsychology, 5
multiplicity, xi, xii, 7, 13, 15
mutual dreams, 35, 37, 45–47
mutual subjectivity, 20, 24, 26, 28,
        32–34, 129–30, 135, 138–39

narcissisism, 52–54, 59, 62, 77, 91,
        105–6, 109–11, 131, 153
nature-nurture, 145–6, 148, 150,
        162, 165

object, 15, 17–18, 26, 30–31, 47,
        61–63, 65–66, 74, 101–103,
        106, 111–12, 115, 128, 149–50
object-relations theory, 15, 17, 20,
        27–31, 36–37, 40, 42, 44, 47,
        49, 57, 68–70, 76, 102, 104,
        106, 146, 151
objectification, 4, 118
one-person psychology, 103–105,
        109
other, 10, 17, 20, 29–32, 47, 61–62,
        64, 70, 91, 93, 130, 142, 144–
        145, 149–50, 155
    otherness, 29, 66, 156

parallel dreaming, 23, 35–37, 39,
        43–47
parallel process, 46, 48–51, 55
paranoid-schizoid position, 12, 29,
        44–45, 69, 152–56
phantasy, 12, 55, 84–85, 89, 93, 98,
        100–101, 107, 114, 119
politics, 144, 151–52
positivism, 18, 26, 33–34, 67, 101,
        133
prenatal, 72–74, 80, 84, 86–90, 93,
        95, 97–98, 100
presentient relatedness, 23, 117–18,
        123–27, 129–30

primitive communication, 35–37, 43,
        47

race, 16, 134, 144, 151–53, 156,
        159–61, 165
    prejudice, 16, 153, 180
reality, objective (external), 4, 63,
        107–8
    psychic (internal), 12, 13, 62,
        107–8
regression, 69–70, 110
relational theory, 1–4, 6, 11–12, 61,
        64, 109, 135
    American relational model(s), 2,
        4–5

sameness, 14, 16–17, 19–20, 102,
        110, 140, 144, 150–151, 155–
        56, 158–159, 165, 178
schizoid, 44, 62, 115
self, 10, 17, 20, 29–32, 45, 47,
        61–64, 66, 71, 73, 79, 91, 93,
        100–101, 106, 115, 120, 125,
        130, 140, 141–42, 144–45, 152,
        154–55
self-in-relation theory, 108
self psychology, 6
separation-individuation, 90–91,
        101, 104–107, 110, 115
set theory, xii, xiii, 13
social constructivism, 5, 7–10, 18,
        20, 108, 146–7, 149, 162
subject, 18, 26–7, 47, 61–3, 65, 74,
        102–3, 111, 115, 128, 149–50
subject-relations, xii, xiii, 18, 25–6,
        28, 30–3, 37, 40, 42, 45, 47, 49,
        57–8, 61, 63, 64, 67, 70, 73,
        89–90, 118, 120, 132, 139, 165
    defined, 21
subjectivity, 4–7, 18, 20–1, 23, 30–2,
        42–4, 58–9, 62, 66–68, 73, 80,
        88–9, 100–1, 112, 117–19, 130,
        133, 136, 165
supervision, 48–59